D1192327

Snow Seen

Well-known as a painter, sculptor and jazz musician, Michael Snow also ranks among the major figures in North American avant-garde film. The enormous success of his 1979 Paris exhibition, in fact, indicates that it is his innovations in film, photography, light and sound that have established him as an artist of international significance.

In this first major study of Snow as filmmaker and photographer, the author places his work within the formalist tradition articulated by such theorists as Malevich, Shklovsky, Léger and Robbe-Grillet, shedding new and fascinating light on the artist's recent work.

REGINA CORNWELL is a New York based critic. She publishes regularly in *Artforum*, has written for other journals including *The Drama Review* and *Studio International*, and has written essays for museum exhibition catalogues. Cornwell has organized film and video exhibitions in the United States and abroad, most recently for the Arts Council of Great Britain. She has taught at the School of Visual Arts, the University of Rochester, Yale, Williams College and Pratt Institute, and has lectured in museums and universities in the U.S., Canada and Europe. She also works actively as a consultant on film and media-related art. Cornwell received her Ph.D. from Northwestern University and has been awarded two National Endowment for the Arts Art Critics' Fellowships.

Photo: Michael Mitchell

Regina Cornwell   **Snow Seen**   The Films and Photographs
of Michael Snow

PMA Books

This book has been published with the help of a grant from the Canadian Federation for the Humanities, using funds provided by the Social Sciences and Humanities Research Council of Canada.

Canadian Cataloguing in Publication Data

Cornwell, Regina
  Snow seen

Bibliography: p.
Filmography: p.
Includes index.

ISBN 0–88778–197–7 bd.

1. Snow, Michael, 1929–   I. Title.

PN1998.A3S56   791.43'0233'0924   C79–094760–9

Design: Michael Solomon

Manufactured in Canada by Webcom Limited

PETER MARTIN ASSOCIATES LIMITED
280 Bloor Street West, Toronto, Canada M5S 1W1

Distributed in the United States by **New York Zoetrope**
31 East 12 Street, New York 10003

Contents

Acknowledgements

This book began in 1973 as a Ph.D. dissertation for Northwestern University. It was completed in 1975 and entitled *Ten Years of Snow*. Since then it has been thoroughly revised and enlarged, as well as retitled. I would like to thank the following individuals and organizations for their help during the long course of my Snow project:

First of all Michael Snow for his generosity and co-operation throughout; Tom Repensek for editing help early on; Jack Ellis, my dissertation advisor at Northwestern; Pierre Théberge, formerly Curator of Contemporary Canadian Art at the National Gallery of Canada and now at the Musée des beaux-arts de Montréal; Joe Medjuck, friend and film advisor for PMA Books; Kathy Vanderlinden, editor at PMA; and of course my publisher, PMA Books; the National Gallery of Canada in Ottawa, the Isaacs Gallery in Toronto and Anthology Film Archives in New York for providing stills; the Film-Makers' Cooperative, the Museum of Modern Art and Castelli-Sonnabend Tapes and Films in New York for use of prints of Snow's films; *Afterimage* (London), *Artforum, Studio International* and the Walker Art Center, Minneapolis (in their *Projected Images* catalogue) which first published articles of mine from which I have quoted .

Finally I want to thank those who have given me their loving support along the way: Peter Wollen, Bill Sloan, Mark Segal, Lauren Ewing, Alice Aycock, Bob Kramer, Meg Shore, and especially Michael Klein and Goldylochs.

Chapter 1

Introducing Snow

There is a famous Russian cartoon in which a hippopotamus, in the bush, points out a zebra to another hippopotamus: "You see," he says, "now that's formalism." The existence of a work of art, its weight, are not at the mercy of interpretative grids which may or may not coincide with its contours.

Alain Robbe-Grillet[1]

For many, Michael Snow's 1969 film *One Second in Montreal* may be a bit like the contours of a zebra: it does not fit precisely into any one interpretive grid. In this film Snow displays the dual tendency, so much a part of his film work since 1964, to couple representational images with means which operate against a simple transparent[2] reading of those images.

One Second in Montreal is representational but is also, in its use of time, abstract. In this case its temporal abstraction is systematic and the film is all of a piece. Though it appears formal, a certain kind of purely formal reading would do it a disservice and would, in fact, be a misreading.

While *One Second* is not concerned per se with defining the differences between film and photography, such differences are implicity and inevitably called to attention because its materials consist of nothing else (beyond the title) but still photographs. Thus another reason for opening this book with *One Second* is that it brings together the two visual media, film and photography, for which Snow is best known today and on which this study focuses. While it is an introduction to his two modes of visual art making, it is also an admittedly recondite and somewhat opaque means of biographical introduction to the artist. Snow does in fact use biographical material in his art in sometimes recondite and sometimes opaque but always in particular and significant ways which I will discuss here briefly and at greater length later.

Snow's twenty-six minute silent film *One Second in Montreal* consists of thirty-one photographs of public spaces in Montreal in winter. This explains the *in Montreal* of the title but why the *One Second*? Snow's answer to this question (calling attention to the two media) is that thirty photographs taken at 1/30 of a second equals one second.

In 1965 these pictures of possible locations for large sculptures were sent to several Canadian artists with an accompanying text

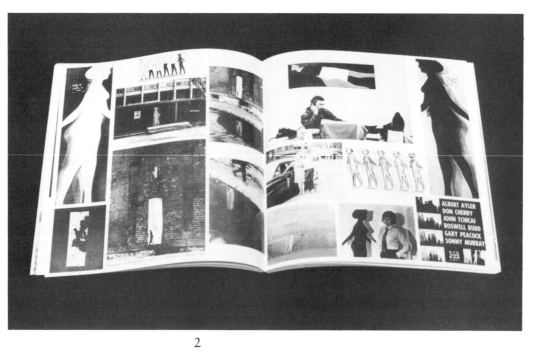

1. *One Second in Montreal*
Photo: Michael Snow

2. *Michael Snow / A Survey*
Photo: T.E. Moore, Isaacs Gallery

describing a sculpture competition they were invited to enter. Snow was one of the sculptors who received the invitation and the pictures. Later he remarked that he had had them "around" for some time. The photographs had been reproduced as offset lithographs and hence were of poor quality, a desirable condition for Snow's use of them in his film—a reproduction at third remove. Originally taken as simple documentation they were, as P. Adams Sitney appropriately points out, "distinctly not artistic photographs."[3] Thus they served Snow as found objects or materials. Here Snow follows in the tradition of Duchamp with his assisted ready-mades, or later, Jasper Johns and Robert Rauschenberg in some of their pieces as he transforms the offset lithographs into material for his art.

At that time, 1965, Snow was best known as a painter and sculptor. His film and photographic work had not yet replaced, let alone seriously challenged, this other work. But between 1965 and 1969 Snow's direction shifted away from painting and sculpture to camera-related work with two major films, *Wavelength* (1966–67) and ⟵⟶ (1968–69), as well as a number of photographic pieces, all of which began to establish his reputation in this area.

In a less obscure autobiographical gesture, for his major retrospective at the Art Gallery of Ontario in Toronto in 1970 Snow produced *Michael Snow / A Survey,* a book which is more than just a catalogue. Snow made of it another work of art by combining the visual and verbal information about his art with photographs of himself, his wife, family and friends taking up various poses or participating in various activities; his family's centuries-old history is represented by a number of ancestral portraits, preceded by a brief note on genealogy. There is a skeletal key mapping out and identifying the pages of unmarked photographs which follow. The book becomes a puzzle which must be pieced together. Some of the puzzle pieces are the snapshots of Lac Clair with the island summer house of Snow's childhood appearing on the cover and punctuating various inside sections. Thus his book is a survey of his life and his art, both treated alike as objects, distanced, as materials for new art.

If *One Second* suggests Snow's past as sculptor, his 1970 book surveys his entire past as artmaker. The repeated reference to the geographical Lac Clair is accompanied by the prominent positioning (as frontispiece) of his 1960 painting *Lac Clair.* Both film and book are reminders of Snow's personal and artistic history, including his early engagements with painting and music.

Michael Snow was born in Toronto in 1929 of an English-Canadian father and a French-Canadian mother. He began painting, drawing and playing music during secondary school at Upper Canada College and then studied design at the Ontario College of Art in Toronto. He first showed his paintings in 1952 in a group exhibition while still a student at the college. After graduation Snow found a job in an advertising agency where he stayed long enough to confirm his complete disinterest in both advertising and design.

After leaving the agency Snow traveled in Europe for a year painting and supporting himself playing jazz piano and trumpet. On his return from Europe in 1955 he had his first major show—a joint exhibition with Graham Coughtry—at Hart House, University of Toronto. George Dunning, later known for his direction of *Yellow Submarine,* saw and liked Snow's paintings and asked him to join his animation department at Graphic Films. It was there that Snow was first exposed to filmmaking, assisting friends on their independent productions and making his own first independent film, an animated work, *A to Z*[4].

Snow remained at Graphic Films for a year and a half (1955–56) and was eventually put in charge of the animation department. When the company went bankrupt he worked freelance on commercial films, played more music and continued to show his work. In 1957 he married artist Joyce Wieland, a former colleague at Graphic Films. His first one-man exhibit was in 1956 at the Isaacs Gallery, then known as the Greenwich Gallery, in Toronto. After a few months sojourn in Cuba in 1957 Snow and Wieland returned to Toronto where he became more involved in music. By 1959 Snow was working as a professional musician.

During that year and the next a change took place in Snow's painting which was to have a bearing on all his later art. His early work had shown the influence of Klee, Matisse and the gestural abstractionists, but now Snow began to move toward non-illusory exploration and became concerned with actual space. In 1959, after the gestural paintings *Secret Shout* and *Blues in Place,* Snow first made the transition to sculpture with *Shunt* and *Quits.* Although both pieces are of painted wood and retain a considerable degree of gesturing, they also assert materiality and begin to move away from the metaphoric and the illusionistic. Perhaps more indicative of the change are the paintings *The Drumbook* (see n.6, chapter 3) and especially *Lac Clair* of the following year. In *The Drumbook* dark blue rectangles rest uneasily on a large yellow-ochre rectangle. Snow's new stress on materials is particularly evident in the single image work so appropriately named *Lac*

Clair, where the flat blue surface is emphasized by strips of ochre paper tape extending from each of the four corners part way along the canvas edge. The blue was mixed with an aluminum paint and the brush strokes though apparent are not impastoed. *Lac Clair,* it is important to note, was titled after the painting was completed.

In their disposal of metaphor these two paintings signal a shift in direction which continued with various ramifications throughout Snow's later work. As Robert Fulford wrote in "Apropos Michael Snow" (echoing Kasimir Malevich): "It would not be too extreme to describe his art over the years as a slow, determined march toward a very special kind of realism: a realism based not on something outside art but rather on the very nature of the art-act itself and on the nature of 'reality' as experienced and as depicted."[5] *Lac Clair* crystallized issues to a greater extent than did *The Drumbook.* In later making it the frontispiece of *A Survey,* Snow seems to have recognized that *Lac Clair* was an important turning point.

Both place and painting are clearly significant for Snow. If in *Lac Clair* Snow was concerned with the tension between image and material which, as Dennis Young suggests, fight for ascendency, both revealing themselves to be what they are,[6] then how does one explain the entry of the "Walking Woman" the following year? Does it entertain some of the same issues and problems or does it veer off into other altogether unrelated areas?

The Walking Woman lived from 1961 to 1967. It existed as replication, series and serial. It was reproduced in painting, drawing, sculpture, film and photography, appeared as decals, stickers and rubber stamps on buildings, in subways and on floors, and was stenciled on ties, sweatshirts and matchbooks, painted on vans and printed in an advertisement in the *Village Voice.* The figure also manifested itself as wallpaper, drapery and as furniture in Snow's apartment in 1963.

The image came originally from a drawing which Snow made from imagination rather than from a model. It is a silhouette of a woman in stride, the feet, hands and crown of her head cropped. The cropping accentuates framing. It may be framed as sculpture, the extremities and crown lost in space, the image drawn in on itself; or it may exist as a painting, photograph or drawing, the extremities and crown apparently cut off by an actual external frame. The model was unchanged until 1963 when Snow made permutations of its original shape and five-foot height—from tiny decal to massive sculpture. In the two-part *Morningside Heights* of 1965 there is only the painted head and upper chest. *Gone* (1963) is a painted relief in which aluminum-painted

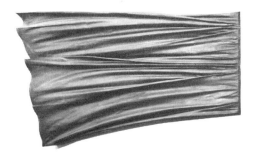

3. *Gone.* Front view.
Photo: John Reeves, Isaacs Gallery

plasticized canvas is stretched across a frame with a Walking Woman profile cut along one projected end. Her image is apparent only when the work is viewed from that end. In *Torso* (1964), a wood and painted canvas construction, part of the Walking Woman is presented rent in torsion, slightly abstracted, the shape still remaining. In *Five Girl Panels* of the same year the image is flattened, fattened, elongated and reduced, more or less of the extremities remaining, the bulk of the trunk increased or reduced in the five separate painted panels. The figure is most often solid white grounded on black or vice versa, although it may be painted in chromatics as is *Morningside Heights* and *Hawaii,* or exist in unpainted metal as in the *Expo Walking Woman.*

Snow has described how the Walking Woman traveled all over the world, taken by friends to Beirut, Caracus, Paris, Moscow and elsewhere and photographically documented in its various surroundings. *Four to Five* (1962) consists of sixteen photographs of the cut-out figure placed in pedestrian locations in streets, subways and buildings. The Walking Woman accompanied Snow and Wieland to New York in the summer of 1963 and took up residence with them there in January 1964.

In some unpublished thoughts on the Walking Woman entitled "A Lot of Near Mrs." (dated 1962–63), Snow writes: "My subject is not women or a woman but the first cardboard cut-out of Walking Woman I made. A second remove depiction.... Walking Woman tho [*sic*] representational, is invented, an individual. One subject, any medium. My work is inclusive not exclusive. Puppetry, choreography. I'm not so interested in making a lot of paintings, sculpture, etc. as finding out what happens when you do such and such a thing.... Trying to find new uses for representation. Not a 'figure painter.' Abstraction of style. Is that possible?"[7]

In *Lac Clair* Snow is concerned with materials and with an anti-illusionist concept of the concrete/abstract synonymous with Malevich's notion of a "new realism" (discussed in the next chapter). In contrast the Walking Woman cut-out is representational. What does Snow mean by "abstraction of style" in the Walking Woman project? Its representational shape is enhanced or diminished; the initial stylized cut-out drawing is stylized again through repetition in series as well as through permutation and variation. In this sense the representational is used abstractly. The figure-subject, a given, frees Snow to concern himself with other issues such as the exploration of media and materials, and questions of form. What happens when the same figure is placed in different environments? What happens when the figure is

4. *Four to Five*
Photo: Michael Snow

multiplied? The persistence of the idea of the Walking Woman in series, serial, replication, and extended over both space and time is most significant in relation to Snow's subsequent film.

Upon arriving in New York Snow felt that he had to make a professional choice between painting and sculpture on the one hand and music on the other; he opted for the former, continuing the Walking Woman project he had begun in Toronto. Film seemed to present no professional conflict at that time and was in fact another vehicle for the Walking Woman. Besides appearing in *Wavelength,* the Walking Woman was to be the basic component of an unfinished film begun in 1962[8] and the central element of *New York Eye and Ear Control* (1964), Snow's second independently made film.

In *New York Eye and Ear Control* Snow's interest in music is still apparent in the strong jazz track which became in 1966 a long-playing album with the same title on ESP label using

7

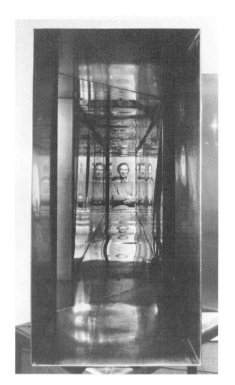

5. *Scope.* The artist is reflected in the sculpture.
Photo: The National Gallery of Canada

Walking Woman images from the film on its dust jacket. Nor did Snow's involvement with music and sound end with that film. In 1967 he did *Sense Solo* for Expo '67, a sound piece using ten simultaneous tapes, in 1969 *Tap,* which has an audio tape, text and photograph, as well as several other audiotape pieces. One of them was *Hearing Aid,* which used cassette tape recorders and a metronome and was first installed at The Kitchen in New York in 1976 and later included in a show, "Another Dimension," at the National Gallery of Canada in Ottawa in 1977. Since his return to Toronto in 1971, Snow's involvement with music has been prodigious. He has been playing piano and trumpet with two improvisational jazz groups in Toronto, Artists' Jazz Band, or AJB, and CCMC. With CCMC he toured across Canada in 1977 and in Europe in May 1978. With each group he has participated in the recording of several LPs. In 1975 he produced on a Chatham Square label a two-record solo album, *Michael Snow: Musics for Piano, Whistling, Microphone and Tape Recorder.* His solo album is related to his other work in terms of ideas and techniques while his participation with AJB and CCMC in improvisation is quite separate and in a different direction.

By 1964 Snow was exhibiting his work at the Poindexter Gallery in New York. A small performance executed at the Film-Makers' Cinematheque entitled *Right Reader* included a taped voice (not Snow's) to which he mimed the words. This piece served as a kind of advertisement for a one-man show at Poindexter in 1965. The tinted transparencies which he held in front of his face in that piece made their way into *Short Shave* (1965), a film which Snow describes as his "worst."[9]

The year that the Walking Woman projects ended with the large stainless steel sculptures called *Expo Walking Woman* for Expo '67, Snow made several other large sculptures, including *Scope* and *First to Last,* both based on the principle of the periscope, and *Sight,* an aluminum and engraved plastic work fitted into a window, containing a large diagonal slit one can look through from either side. All of these sculptures make clear, in one manner or another, the growing effect of the camera on Snow's work since *New York Eye and Ear Control.* As Snow stated in 1967, "For the last three or four years, I have been influenced by films and by the camera. When you narrow down your range and are looking through just that narrow aperture of the lens, the intensity of what you see is so much greater."[10]

In 1967 Snow also completed the photographic works *Snow Storm, February 7, 1967* and *Atlantic.* At the same time that he was conceiving and designing the Expo sculptures he was also reflecting on *Wavelength.* After actively thinking about it for a year, Snow shot the film in one week in December 1966, and first showed the final edited print in May 1967. It was Jonas Mekas's encouragement that persuaded Snow to send a print to the film festival in Knokke-le-Zoute, where it took the $4,000 grand prize for 1967–68. Thus 1966–67 marked the end of one phase in Snow's career and the beginning of another as the Walking Woman gave way to a serious commitment to filmmaking.

New films followed in fairly rapid succession after *Wavelength*. *Standard Time* (1967), an eight-minute work employing a panning camera, is a study for the following fifty-four minute film ←——→ , begun in 1968 and completed in 1969. That same year, along with his *One Second in Montreal,* Snow collaborated with Joyce Wieland on *Dripping Water,* followed the next year by his *Side Seat Paintings Slides Sound Film.* All three use a stationary camera. The long and complex film of constant camera movement *La Région Centrale* was finished in 1971. Using the tracking shot Snow next filmed *Breakfast,* a.k.a. *Table Top Dolly,* in 1972 which he put aside and returned to complete in 1976. Another version of this work, made in 1972, was a transfer from film to videotape entitled *Three Breakfasts.* It consists of three successive tracking shots on the thirty-minute video tape. After more than two years of work, in the fall of 1974 Snow completed his four-hour-twenty-minute *"Rameau's Nephew" by Diderot (Thanx to Dennis Young) by Wilma Schoen,* dedicated to Alexander Graham Bell. It marks somewhat of a departure from his earlier work and is a concentrated radical examination of the possibilities of sound in terms of music, speech and language—an area previously little explored in film. While Snow was still editing *"Rameau's Nephew"*. . .he started to film *Two Sides to Every Story,* shot with two cameras, the projection situation essentially isomorphic to the making situation with the projectors placed where the cameras had been and a two-sided screen in the centre of the gallery space. This was made specifically for a group exhibition entitled "Projected Images" at the Walker Art Center, Minneapolis, in the fall of 1974.

His film and non-film works have been shown in one-man and group shows in Canada, the United States and abroad. In 1970 Snow was chosen to represent Canada in the Thirty-fifth Venice Biennial. The same year his films were exhibited at the Cannes Film Festival. He was given a film retrospective at Pesaro, Italy in 1972 and at the Cinémathèque québécoise in Montreal in 1975. Also in 1972 he had a large and significant show of photographic slide, video, sound and film pieces entitled "About 30 Works by Michael Snow" at the Center for Inter-American Relations in New York where the machine used in the making of *La Région*

Centrale was mounted with a video camera in a work named *De La*. In 1976 he had a complete retrospective of his films along with a show of his photographs at the Museum of Modern Art in New York. An exhibition entitled "Michael Snow: Sept films et *Plus Tard*" (this last a photographic installation of 1977) was organized at the Centre Georges Pompidou in Paris and traveled through France in 1977 and 1978. This was followed by a major exhibition of film, photography and sculpture at the Centre Pompidou in December 1978 which subsequently toured Switzerland, Holland, Germany and Canada, ending in Vancouver in early 1980. After leaving the Poindexter Gallery in New York, Snow showed briefly with Jon Gibson and then with the Bykert Gallery for several years. In Toronto he continues to exhibit with Isaacs Gallery. He has received three Canada Council Grants, the most recent one in 1973–74 for *"Rameau's Nephew".*, and a Guggenheim Fellowship in 1972. Snow's films are collected in archives internationally. Since 1971 he and Wieland have been living in Toronto after their eight-year stay in New York.

How does biography play into his work? As pointed out earlier, in *One Second in Montreal* the reclaimed photographs carry an allusion to Snow as sculptor. *Michael Snow/A Survey* is autobiographical yet distanced with the images finally saying more about his art than his life. These are but two of many examples of in one case an abstruse and in the other an apparent use of autobiography.

What is significant is that while Snow uses his biography over and over as material for his art, the art provides no access to his life. His biography in some senses, like his art, resists romanticization. And his art as a whole, though it uses formal devices, eludes rigidly formalized critical readings.

The resistance to romantic as well as to extremely formal readings and, as shall be explored, the distances set up through the work itself, whether it incorporates biographical material or not, may seem like quite separate issues, but in fact are connected in terms of placing Show within a critical-historical framework.

One Second in Montreal is a convenient pivotal point. Snow once spoke of his double working consideration in filmmaking: on the one hand time and systems of duration, and on the other materials which are at the same time different yet similar. In *One Second* as in Snow's other work, going at least as far back as his Walking Woman up to but not including *"Rameau's Nephew".*, there is this restriction to and exploration of one subject. Here each of the photographs is different yet all have the same subject matter—public spaces possible for sculpture. And, as they are all

10

slightly pale due to the bleak, wintry ambience and to their reproduction from photography to offset lithography to film, their overall homogeneous look is formally enhanced and they become more explicitly all of a piece.

The emphasis on time operates in several ways through Snow's two-part system of duration. During the first half of the film the time that each image is on the screen increases in regular units, and in the second it regularly decreases, using a different arithmetic notation, down to the single last frame. The images are fixed; however, distinctly unlike the standard and commercial uses of the frozen frame, here there is neither a visual nor a voice-over narration. In fact there is no sound at all to interfere with the time measured over the space of the film and to draw away from the immediacy of the temporal experience of the film-object. In *One Second in Montreal,* time itself is stressed.

Snow's method of emphasizing time inevitably calls to attention the differences between viewing a photograph and viewing a film. A photograph is customarily seen in the perceiver's own time whereas here the single frames are transferred to motion picture frames seen through the filmmaker's designated time within the conditions of the projection process, so that the stasis of photography paradoxically persists and is hyperbolized in the movement of the ribbon of film. Here the photographs become, in a sense, frozen in time and out of place, or to use Victor Shklovsky's term, which shall be considered later, they are *defamiliarized.*

Even while Snow uses the "window" or illusionistic aspect of the found materials he seems to contain or restrict them. That is, through the overall thematic and visual coherence of the shots and through the a priori time scheme which he imposes upon them, Snow formalizes the film. Within this scheme the images appear for increasing and then decreasing durations, but one realizes that this system suggests no hierarchy of value as far as the images themselves are concerned. Instead, the viewing experience lies purely in the perception of time and is about time as it falls back upon itself. The content is a fragmentary or inchoate narrative, yet paradoxically the concept and formalization of the film shape another kind of content: while using the world as subject, the film at the same time cuts itself off from it, turning it in upon itself as the material for art.

"Windows to the world," "capturing and recording raw reality", are just two phrases common in popular and conservative film criticism. But it can't be supposed even at a superficial glance that *One Second in Montreal* is and does these things. The casual, unformalized images, mysterious and ambiguous, would

11

seem perfect material for a humanist reading of cinema. But the form which *One Second* takes militates against a humanist reading of the film in the vein of André Bazin or Siegfried Kracauer (discussed in chapter 2). *One Second in Montreal* demonstrates the practical inadequacies of a realistic prescriptive theory of film and indicates something of a critical dilemma in film criticism. Bazin's humanist approach offers no access to *One Second,* which will appear opaque, inadequate and incomplete from such a position.

While a traditional humanist position is untenable, so is a reductivist formal interpretation in the Anglo-American critical tradition of, for instance, a Clive Bell or a Clement Greenberg which would ignore or reject the importance of the photographs as reclaimed objects, overlook context and attempt to come to some essentialist position about the film's form. Both do a disservice to *One Second in Montreal* and to Snow's work in general. The issue is to find an adequate critical context in which to consider Snow's work. This inevitably leads to a search outside of the sphere of film into critical methods from both the visual arts and literature. Some of these will be taken up in the next chapter before continuing in subsequent chapters to concentrate on specific works.

Chapter 2

Sources

Of *Wavelength* Gene Youngblood wrote exuberantly, "It is a triumphant and definitive answer to André Bazin's seminal question: "Qu'est-ce que le cinéma?"[1]

But would Bazin have thought so? Certainly not. Neither *Wavelength* nor *One Second in Montreal* nor any of Snow's other works answer to Bazin's conservative and established theory and criticism on the nature of cinema as a realistic medium. There is also Siegfried Kracauer's *Theory of Film,* first published in 1960, before Bazin was in translation in North America. While Bazin poses the question, Kracauer seems immediately to answer it in the very subtitle of his book: *The Redemption of Physical Reality,* spelling out his similarly conservative position from the start. However, it is for more than polemical reasons that I introduce this chapter with Bazin's questioning title and Kracauer's apparently complementary answer. This mode of critical thought has been and remains influential. In some recent academic studies, semiotics led by Christian Metz seems to have supplanted the theories of Bazin; but even that is questionable for there is the notion that Metz's early work continues Bazin's thought in more systematic ways.[2] There is also, among others, Stanley Cavell's *The World Viewed: Reflections on the Ontology of Film.* And precedents can easily be found in the past for attitudes and assumptions about cinema which return it to its origins in order to explore its nature. The eminent art historian Erwin Panofsky wrote one essay on cinema, "Style and Medium in the Motion Pictures" (1934), a piece often referred to as an acknowledged influence on Cavell. The position espoused by Bazin at his best and most eloquent is present also in more pedestrian forms which permeate popular reviews and writing about cinema. Though Bazin's and Kracauer's writing predate *Wavelength* and Snow's other important films, Cavell's text was published when Snow was well into his film career.

As has been mentioned, Snow commented that the act of looking through the camera—the framing process—made him begin to see things differently. His sculpture was influenced. Finally his entire visual oeuvre was dominated by the products of movie and still camera and camera processes.

The looking through is hardly a passive process for Snow. Whereas for Bazin in *What Is Cinema?* and also for Kracauer in *Theory of Film: The Redemption of Physical Reality* the nature of the camera and picture-taking itself becomes passive. The camera for Bazin is an automatic instrument able to record and reveal reality without human interference or manipulation. Movies go beyond stills in adding the aspect of motion, and in proceeding toward fulfilling man's aspiration for a myth of total cinema, a total realism.[3] Not that the camera is competing with the other arts but instead is simply assuming a function of recording in ways the other arts cannot, in so doing freeing painting and sculpture to pursue different ends. The camera records, according to Bazin, not in mere trompe-l'oeil fashion, by substituting for reality, but by fulfilling man's spiritual and aesthetic desire for realism. This is made possible through the indexical[4] aspect of the recording process which transfers reality like a "fingerprint."[5] "Photography affects us like a phenomenon in nature, like a flower or a snowflake whose vegetable or earthly origins are an inseparable part of their beauty," he writes.[6]

In a much less eloquent and sophisticated fashion, Kracauer refers to photography and film as arts "with a difference."[7] For him they are totally separate from the traditional arts. Because of the instantaneousness of the camera's operation, equivalent to Bazin's automatism, photography and film are not formal; this is what underlies the separation from the other arts which are formal and which are affected by formal concerns.[8]

In both critical instances the separateness of the camera process, its automatism or instantaneousness, is the rationale for a realism. And from that realism follow types of narrative supported by a stylistic transparency. In Bazin there is a concern for, yet a definite vacillation about, form. But in both Bazin's and Kracauer's work finally this is form subservient to content, one which abjures abstraction. In the end both writers are trumpeting a type of humanism or neohumanism, an art disguising itself, revealing and recording the world but not questioning it, not constructing or deconstructing it, only taking it in intact. Thus the art, the film, becomes a grand gestalt equivalent to the world.

It is no surprise that their critical choices converge on the Italian neorealists in whose work can be seen a connection between humanism and neorealism.[9] For Kracauer both photography and film are basically "material aesthetics," meaning that their content is what is most important, ignoring form. Through his idea of the instantaneousness of the camera medium he equates "camera reality" with "material reality," "physical existence" and "actuality" so that in a circular fashion a material aesthetics becomes what is natural.[10] Bazin, despite his claim, is however much less concerned finally with a superficial mimesis than with the means and process of recording, of capturing, of

14

transferring a sense of totality and a feeling for reality.

Bazin and Kracauer view film as a popular art with no room for an avant-garde, as does Erwin Panofsky in his "Style and Medium in the Motion Pictures." He sees its origins derived from the popular folk arts of the last century. Codified in the film of the first decade of this century, the genres and character types of the primitive film are developed with new technology but remain essentially the same. For Panofsky, as for Bazin and Kracauer, film's medium is "physical reality as such," and style comes from the surreptitious manipulation of reality without prestylization but "in such a way that the result has style."[11] Genres and character types become for Panofsky the consequences and manifestations of style, but formal considerations are taboo for they are a part of prestylization.

The "nature" of the medium and the "naturalism" of the recording processes are the bases on which these conservative theories are built. As description, part of what Panofsky says is in fact quite true: genres and character types were codified early in the primitive state of the medium, changing little over time. But, perhaps ironically, what he praises in his prescription as the only kind of film is at the same time commercial film—highly transparent, low risk, high box-office products, prime commodities of a conservative business community and entertainment system. In film he seems to see no place for an art which he describes as being made at "the creative urge of its maker."[12]

Panofsky does not admit artistic or other value in attempts to break away from fixed classical genres. Of course, Panofsky, interested in iconography, is writing in Hollywood's heyday, in the wake of the 1920s avant-garde, the very year of Jean Vigo's death and four years after *L'Age d'Or*'s appearance and virtual disappearance. Describing the mainstream, he is not interested in offering predictive alternatives as he praises the value of film as mass communication over the non-commercial and possibly recondite film.

However, aesthetician Stanley Cavell, whose *The World Viewed: Reflections on the Ontology of Film* appeared in 1971, was not writing in the wave of a film avant-garde.[13] Even though he seems to possess an awareness of relatively contemporary art, at least up through minimalism, he chooses either to dismiss or for the most part to ignore totally the very active film avant-garde and to centre his attentions on the commercial cinema. While Cavell borrows heavily from Bazin and Panofsky, in his writing there is a curious and ambiguous breakthrough as he strives to fashion a modernist position for film, the tenets of which are largely taken from art critics Clement Greenberg and Michael

15

Fried. But he fails in his formulation precisely because he attempts a merger with Bazin and Panofsky. Modernism's considerations seem always to begin with an avant-garde, as certain of Greenberg's writings are witness to.[14] In contrast, Cavell, in tailoring his theory and use of modernism to the needs of the entertainment film, appears to miss the point, for in its practice and theory modernism is not destined to accommodate comfortably such popular commercial art.

Through an unexamined set of expectations and assumptions, Cavell and the others enforce for all film a hierarchy of values and positions about art and culture inherited from the Renaissance but long actively fought against by twentieth-century artists and critics working in other fields. These values may indeed be applied to popular film, but not all film is popular. Snow's film work is part of an avant-garde and therefore not within the vein of the popular and easily accessible. If one looks outside the literature on film to that on the other arts, one finds modernist and post-modernist traditions in which Snow's film and photographic work can be located and understood. In these movements terms such as *form, object, abstraction, discontinuity, deformation* and *defamiliarization* hold their critical places against sometimes outraged charges of dehumanization, and the *real* and *new realism* are used in ways totally unlike the general realism or the specific neorealism of Bazin and Kracauer.[15]

José Ortega y Gasset observes in his *Dehumanization of Art* that modernism, or as he put it in 1925, modern art or the new art, is hardly in a position of popular and commercial esteem. (While he does not use the expression *avant-garde*, clearly his terms are interchangeable with it.) He examines the polarization in the arts of the two decades prior to his writing. Proceeding from the outside in—from the audience to the art—the philosopher classifies the new work as being not merely not popular but also unpopular and anti-popular. Such new art stands in contrast to romanticism, whose works, according to Ortega y Gasset, "were the first, after the invention of printing, to enjoy large editions. Romanticism was the prototype of a popular style. First born of democracy, it was coddled by the masses." However, he continues, "modern art on the other hand, will always have the masses against it."[16]

Yet as Renato Poggioli points out in *Theory of the Avant-Garde*, both bourgeois democracy and romanticism are historically connected in important ways to the avant-garde. Political democracy was a prerequisite for romanticism, which in turn helped pave the way for an avant-garde. Classicism upheld work rooted in mastery and method, tradition and authority, so that repetition of the "stencil"—the "eternal maxims of ancient wisdom"—was an accepted practice.[17] Romanticism broke through all of this. Lauding dynamism and innovation, it assumed a popularity. However, the avant-garde, which is also propelled by a dynamism in which originality is significant and the sterotype frowned upon, enjoys no such popular place.[18]

The romanticism of the nineteenth century became popular, according to Ortega y Gasset, because it exulted "lived reality" and transparency, and upheld the illusion that little distinction exists between life and art, so that the latter merely breaks down the barrier between the two. But the new arts stand in distinction to such "cross-eyed art," as he characterizes the art of the last century. Although democracy was necessary for the production and the very existence of both romantic and avant-garde art, with the avant-garde there is an inversion of audience reaction. The new arts no longer nurture access by a mass audience; a minority group, privy to and concerned with understanding its less available and often recondite motivations and sensibilies, becomes its public. The new artists, aware that older forms are exhausted, focus their attentions not on "lived reality" but on artistic form. Ortega y Gasset draws the conclusion that to do this such art derealizes reality and dehumanizes the human, moving in this way toward abstraction.

Early in the twentieth century T. E. Hulme in his vociferous opposition to romanticism "Classicism and Romanticism" prophesies a return to classicism in the arts.[19] By this he means a movement away from "the circumambient gas" of romanticism with its proclivity for "soft" metaphors and its claims for man's unlimitedness. He relegates such flights of the imagination to the hereafter and sees the return to the classical ideal as a "recognition" of finitude with the "hard and dry" language of the new poetry asserting the concrete in the here and now. What is occurring in art in this pre-World War I period during which Hulme writes is not, of course, a renaissance of classicism. But this prediction of a return to the finite in art combined with a concern for change and innovation inherited from romanticism creates a different aesthetic in which terms such as classicism and romanticism in themselves no longer have a place.

But there is another important increment to account for. Ortega y Gasset hints at it when he refers to modern art as an "artist's art"; Cavell writes of it in *The World Viewed;* and Clement Greenberg speaks of it on more than one occasion. It is the idea of an art questioning itself and calling attention to its own procedure. Pre-romantic occidental art had its window-like perspectival public view. In romanticism this window becomes

17

mirror and perspective shifts to the privacy of the artist's soul. In much of twentieth-century art there is a move away from subjective and soul-searching reflection to a focus on the materials and processes of the art itself.[20] This tendency toward reflexivity has accelerated over recent decades undergoing changes with minimal art in the mid-1960s followed by conceptual and post-conceptual art.

The issues of finitude, innovation, change and an art questioning and reflecting on itself highlight an art as well as a body of critical methods which as part of modernism tend to draw attention to the surface of the object or event itself, and also more recently to the relationship or transaction between object and perceiver. I discreetly note "part of modernism" since the movement is broad and encompassing.[21] Here I am concerned with formal issues of modernism and with what leads into postmodernism.[22]

There is art which is formal. There is art which may be viewed above all for its particular formal properties or characteristics. And there is formal method and criticism. It is this last which is the subject of this chapter.

Within art circles in the United States, all formal criticism and method tends unfortunately and mistakenly to be collapsed into one and equated with the name Clement Greenberg and to a lesser extent his younger colleagues, especially Michael Fried. And the terms *formalism* and *formalist* are frequently used pejoratively—against both certain kinds of art production and certain modes of criticism. This formalist tradition goes back to Clive Bell and Roger Fry in England. In criticizing Greenberg one gains a better perspective by first analyzing the positions of Fry and Bell which are certainly open to much question. In the visual arts the connections between them and Greenberg are striking. A further link in terms of sensibility and attitude is the work of the New Critics, or Southern Critics, who were part of a formalism in literature. Appearing in America in the thirties and forties, they were strongly influenced by I.A. Richards in England and Anglo-American T.S. Eliot.

But it must be stressed that this is only one kind of formalism. Another distinctly different kind can be traced back to Kasimir Malevich and Victor Shklovsky in Russia and others on the continent. The differences between them and the Anglo-American critics are significant and all too seldom called to attention. It is within this continental tradition of formalist theory that I will later locate the work of Michael Snow.

If today Greenberg's thinking seems restricted, so does that of Roger Fry and especially Clive Bell, both contemporaries and fellow countrymen of T.E. Hulme. An examination of historical events makes clear why they maintain such narrow places. As George Kubler writes in *The Shape of Time:* "An important component in historical sequences of artistic events is an abrupt change of content and expression at intervals when an entire language form suddenly falls into disuse, being replaced by a new language of different components and an unfamiliar grammar. An example is the sudden transformation of occidental art and architecture about 1910. . . . as if large numbers of men had suddenly become aware that the inherited repertory of forms no longer corresponded to the actual meaning of existence."[23]

With the shift toward abstraction Fry and Bell came to see how acutely a new language was needed. Fry observed that painting had been valued too often for its subject matter or content which he referred to as its extra-aesthetic or non-aesthetic element. Now both critics concerned themselves with changing the focus of attention from subject matter to form in order to deal with the evolving new art and with older work as well. Concerning his Post-Impressionist Exhibition at the Grafton Galleries in London in 1910, Roger Fry asserted that the work displayed there continued a line of concern with form as part of a heritage from the greatest of the past masters. But the public scoffed at this, recognizing no such continuity in the art of Gaugin, Cézanne, Van Gogh and others included.

Bell, assimilating the thought of his older colleague, attempted to push further, establishing a broad and general theory for painting and sculpture whose two axes were "significant form" and "aesthetic emotion." In a painting, Bell writes, "lines and colour combined in a particular way, certain forms and relations of forms, stir our aesthetic emotions. These relations and combinations of lines and colours, these aesthetically moving forms, I call 'Significant Form.' "[24]

In reacting against obsolete methods inapplicable to modern work and against the spectator's tendency to concentrate on subject matter or content, Bell swings to the opposite pole. He insists that all that is needed to appreciate significant form is an understanding of line, colour, form and space, and all that matters is significant form joined to aesthetic emotion. Through this form-emotion partnership Bell finally repudiates intellect which he sees connected with content as the informational matter of representational painting. Here intellect and content mean only the extra-aesthetic in Bell's quest for the object of attention.[25] Traces of this position are present in Greenberg.

Bell's book, *Art,* becomes dogmatic. While he purports to be open to representation it is clear he is not from his off-hand remark that "not every picture is as good seen upside down as upside up" and his argument that there is only good and bad art, the latter having insignificant form and consequently inferior quality because it focuses on material beauty and daily emotion.[26] With such attitudes one can see how formalism, to the degree that it is understood and filtered through Bell and to a lesser extent Fry, has come pejoratively to mean design and decoration, and a formalist someone of rare aesthetic sensibility able to see lines, colours and form in arrangements upside down and upside up.

The extremes of the two writers often overshadow what is most important in their contributions to critical and artistic thought. They must be seen in historical perspective. When Bell asks if " 'significant form' isn't what philosophers used to call 'the thing in itself' and now call 'ultimate reality,' " he begins to sound like an idealist and comes dangerously close to obscuring his goal: to name that element present in a work as "end in itself."[27] For Bell a work's significant form is its reality and its end in itself. In spite of the severe limitations of his theory of significant form, Bell does seek to locate attention on what is in the work of art itself. But more clearly and articulately than his colleagues, Fry conveys this concept of reality in the new arts in an essay written in 1912. "The fact is, that the average man uses art entirely for its symbolic value. Art is in fact the symbolic currency of the world . . . but in a world of symbolists the creative artist and the creative man of science appear in strange isolation as the only people who are not symbolists. They alone are up against certain relations which do not stand for something else, but appear to have ultimate value, to be real."[28] Their concepts of the object in itself and the realism of the new arts also connect Bell and Fry with the other direction of formalism, as shall be seen later.

As well as writing for art magazines, in the thirties and forties Clement Greenberg published articles in such periodicals as *Partisan Review, The Nation* and *The New Leader.* Under these liberal leftist banners he was a strong spokesman for modern and contemporary art. It was in the 1960s, beginning with the highly influential essay "Modernist Painting" of 1961, that Greenberg's role as critic became controversial and for at least the next ten years late modernism in art and theory bore the traces of his ideas. His initially dynamic role finally became a rigid and rather destructive one promoting a flaccid and academic art.

In "Modernist Painting" Greenberg explains modernism historically as a cultural-artistic movement inheriting the self-critical tendency from Kantian thinking of the eighteenth century. This self-criticism, now applied to literature, painting, sculpture and the other arts, means seeking an art's irreducible limits, the materials of each medium distinguishing it from other media, straining each out to a purity. He writes: "Realistic, naturalistic art had dissembled the medium, using art to conceal art; modernism used art to call attention to art. The limitations that constitute the medium of painting—the flat surface, the shape of the support, the properties of pigment—were treated by the old masters as negative factors that could be acknowledged only implicitly or indirectly. Under modernism these same limitations came to be regarded as positive factors, and were acknowledged openly."[29]

Concerned in these essays of the early sixties with abstract expressionism and post-painterly abstraction, he claims, in effect, as does Bell, not to be opposed to representation. Painting is about the depiction of space in two dimensions, without sculptural illusion, yet like Bell he finally is not sympathetic to representation in new art. In observing his ideas put to artistic and critical practice over a period of time by others, one sees that the stress he places on self-criticism, on the search for the purity of the medium in an abstraction totally dismissing representation, is taken literally and figuratively farther than he wished to see it go. Minimal art is an example. He attacks it as totally unacceptable. But indeed it is an inevitable consequence or a parody of his ideas, while it is also a reaction to them.

But where is form in all of this? Where are the irreducible qualities of each medium? By 1971 Greenberg has reduced form to artisanry strained through the refinements of taste. There is so much work within the areas of post-painterly abstraction and other new painting, Greenberg argues, that artisanry is necessary for form, but good taste will separate out quality from quantity.[30] The artisanry, if of good quality, will be informed by inspiration, he continues—so as not to make it all too cut and dried. Greenberg's terms seem to repeat Bell's aesthetic emotion and significant form in other ways.

It is Greenberg's reductivism which is disturbing. While he does hold to a continuation within modernism of ideas from an older tradition, part of that continuity is achieved by the virtual exclusion of certain styles and certain media (such as film and photography) which represent ruptures and discontinuities of which he disapproves. For him Duchamp and Dada are simply destructive, facile and puerile attempts to avoid the problems of form, and through this avoidance also jettison the issue of quality.

He writes: "The quality of art depends on inspired, felt relations or proportions as on nothing else. There is no getting around this. A simple, unadorned box can succeed as art by virtue of these things; and when it fails as art it is not because it is merely a plain box, but because its proportions, or even its size, are uninspired, unfelt. The same applies to works in any other form of 'novelty' art: kinetic, atmospheric, light, environmental, 'earth', 'funky', etc. etc."[31] He imposes the same nebulous, purely subjective standards on all art, and in so doing inevitably must exclude much of it for not fulfilling his taste criteria. Greenberg's orthodoxy finally accommodates very little.

Despite some valuable insights, Greenberg's writings began to reflect a conservatism and a closure. Historical reasons can be found for Fry's and Bell's critical constructions but Greenberg's cul de sac is less defensible. However, it does historically parallel, even as it helps bring about, the demise of modernism in the visual arts.[32]

From the beginning the New Critics were conservative. John Crowe Ransom was a leader of the Southern Agrarian movement and a teacher at Vanderbilt University where his later colleagues and the key practitioners of the New Criticism Allen Tate, Cleanth Brooks and Robert Penn Warren were first his students.[33] While they were politically conservative, their methods at the time of development in the late thirties and forties were critically and artistically advanced. They opposed a prevailing neohumanism which reduced literature to biography, history, sociology or politics while they sought to maintain the work's autonomy, reading it for what it was in itself. In this way they were trying to recuperate a knowledge which was indeed an aesthetic knowledge outside scientific and positivistic thought. Why go to poetry, they asked, to attain a knowledge better available from another source? Poetry had something else to offer, something important to life but separate from it.

The lyric, small and by its nature enclosed, was the special purview of the New Critics. Irony, metaphor, literary tropes were their devices for examining poetic language. The movement, more and more academicized, continued actively in the United States into the early 1960s when it was subject to ever increasing attack by various schools wanting to go beyond formalism. By that time it had exerted an influence, both positive and negative, on the reading habits and analytical methods of many graduates and undergraduates of those times.[34]

Murray Krieger in his *The New Apologists for Poetry* explains well the complex position of the Southern Critics who were often accused of an "art for art's sake" stance:

Thus while refusing to subjugate literature to science or to philosophy by giving it the function of illuminating general truths, these "new critics" had equally to eschew an "art for art's sake" position which would trivialize literature. They had somehow to assert at once the autonomy of art and its unique power to give meaning to our experience, a power allowed only by its autonomy. This is a highly significant, if difficult, assertion. It can be understood only if we first abandon the common misconception which, insisting that an autonomous art can only be one practiced for its own sake, identifies "the new criticism" precisely with this dilettantism of the aesthete.[35]

But Geoffrey Hartman in *Beyond Formalism* urges a look at the value system lauded by the New Critics, at how their politics does indeed shade their critical position, pulling at its advanced or radical parts. Unity, order, organicism, lack of conflict within the poem—all are reminiscent of another world indeed. Hartman writes:

It is important not to be deceived by the sophisticated vagueness of such terms as *unit, complexity, maturity, coherence,* which enter criticism at this point. They are code words shored against the ruins. They express a highly neoclassical and acculturated attitude; a quiet nostalgia for the ordered life; and a secret recoil from aggressive ideologies, substitute religions, and dogmatic concepts of order. Out of the passionate intensity of the post-war period—out of the pressures of politics, press and propaganda—comes a thoughtful backlash which attempts to distinguish the suasion of literary statements from more imperative kinds.[36]

Certain preoccupations of the New Critics are shared by a leading exponent of the second, continental school of formalist thought. Their differences, however, are striking and significant.

Malevich, founder of suprematism,[37] whose *Essays on Art*[38] were begun before the Russian Revolution of 1917 and continued until 1933, two years before his death, expresses in his writings an energy shared by the constructivists and futurists of that early revolutionary period, yet he does not participate in their desire to break down the barrier between art and life so that art might, in utilitarian agit-prop fashion, serve the new Soviet state. While he speaks of the separation of art from economics and social pressure, he also holds that each art must draw from its own culture and its own time and not regress to the past. In his bombastic fashion he writes of the reactionary art of this day: "Their bodies fly in aeroplanes, but art and life are covered with the old robes of Neroes and Titians." And, "the technical side of our age forges further and further ahead, but art tries to draw us further and further back" (1:21-22). Even more succinctly, "The transferring of real objects onto canvas is the art of skillful reproduction, and only that" (1:24). This, he argues, is to paint illusion—the illusion of a prior time and prior space, and to transport the viewer and distract his perceptions from what

23

actually exists on canvas in two dimensions. The new painting, he proclaims, is concerned with no such illusion of reality; it is the new realism of a nonobjective world concerned with line, colour, form, with "painterly-as-suchness" and the sensations conveyed. He disposes of traditional mimesis by suggesting that man as part of nature is free to create whatever forms he desires. He can perceive and use nature as material mass so that the end result has nothing to do with nature. On this point he agrees with Bell who maintains that the artist may go to nature to arrive at pure form.

Malevich replaces the traditional form-content dichotomy with a triadic distinction: form, content and subject. His is a somewhat more sophisticated attempt to deal with the problem. Form becomes a condition, and subject, the matter outside the work—that illusion of prior or otherwise existing reality. Calling the new arts "basically subjectless," he continues, "but this does not mean that they have no content or that they represent only formal searchings; we see for example in Cézanne's works the painterly content which outweighs the content of the subject's significance" (2:27-28). While he speaks of intuition and not reason as the creative force in art, he is singling out utilitarian reason. Art is about "intuitive reasoning," and as he writes in "A Letter to the Dutch Artists" (1922), "Art has its own content in its ideas" (1:185). Bell and to a large degree Fry, in spite of his protests, felt the need to repudiate the intellect in art, allying content with the intellect and salvaging the work through significant form and its accompanying aesthetic emotion which come out of perception and sensation. Greenberg also undermines intellect in acts of making and responding to painting, championing intuition, while the New Critics, similarly to Malevich, hold to a special kind of knowledge in art, separate from that attainable from science. In contrast to the more passive, pleasurable emotion of art promulgated by Bell, Malevich maintains that through intuitive reasoning art creates the higher life of the nonobjective world—a new world and reality, forms generating new forms, growing and changing. These new forms emerge from the tenor of the times. They parallel man's search through utilitarian reason for new means of political, economic and social expression and new structures in industry. This art, Malevich argues, like the new century in which it is finding its beginnings, is shaking off traditions from the past, and consequently the perceptions which it calls for are very much a part of the demands of its times. "It is only by forming signs of our creation that we advance and move away from the past, and therefore we cannot establish eternal beauty with our new inventions"(1:85).

Here Malevich and the Russian formalists along with the futurists and cubists part company with the conservativism of the New Critics. While these early movements all extolled science and looked to its energy in the new arts as sign of a new culture and society, the New Critics saw science as an enemy and art as a bastion against assaults on sensitivity and holism, a means of preserving traditional values so that finally art and form were moral devices. Greenberg in his positive reference to science argues for the artfulness of the art object or the literariness of literature. Science is a paradigm in that it allows a thing to be examined on its own terms and considered in and for itself, an attitude espoused by Malevich but one he did not employ to extend his position about the art object in itself.

Malevich considers the art beginning with the impressionists, including Cézanne and the cubists and leading to his own suprematist movement, as a new realism. He wants viewers to see this art as it is in its own time and space without perceiving it as symbol. While Fry, Bell and Greenberg want emphatically to separate out the aesthetic from the non-aesthetic in the perception of art, Malevich explains that aesthetic is generally identified in the minds of most people with "beauty," illusion and classical art and he rejects these meanings, maintaining that the new arts "do not contain images and objects having an artistic side" but are concerned with generating energy and with other sensations not previously thought of as artistic (2:121). Greenberg maintains the meaning of aesthetic, Bell and Fry seek to change it, while Malevich seizes upon and analyzes its old connotations in order to place them against the fresh meanings and experiences available in modern works of art. He, Bell and Fry are concerned with the same task although they pursue it from different directions. Finally, however, Malevich opens up greater possibilities through his more provocative approach.

Form, energy, sensation and feeling are words which pepper Malevich's vocabulary: the sensation, for instance, of dynamism—man's energy and the energy of new forms which one feels. "The world which is understood by sensation is a constant world. The world which consciousness understands as a form is not constant. Forms disappear and alter, whereas sensations neither disappear nor alter. A ball, motor, aeroplane or arrow are different forms, but the sensation of dynamism is the same" (2:138).

The stress on energy and sensation, and on form "as a condition" which in actuality does not exist, leads Malevich into a wholesale idealism. He asserts that form is not attached to matter because matter does not exist; only energy exists and energy "comprises what we call body"(1:223). Malevich would probably not wish to be called a formalist per se, for he writes near the end of his second volume: "The formal method discovers the forms of phenomena, but not their reality or spirit (if I may put it thus). For form, colour and spirit are phenomena with different states of energy" (2:139). The energy of sensations comprises a constant universe for Malevich but within this universe forms change.

Yet out of Malevich's idealism form "as a condition" emerges as a necessary prerequisite for another triadic system which is very important in his thinking. It consists of the *invariable forming*, the *supplementary forming,* and the *deforming* elements. The invariable forming element is described as the objective mark or style of a school or movement, and the supplementary as the individual artist's style within the larger school. But of most significance in this context is the deforming element which he characterizes in two ways: historically (for example, "it is called deforming if the relations of the elements in Cubism are reconstructed into Suprematism" [1:12]); and individually (for instance, the artist moves away from illusion "altering the form for the sake of perceiving painterly elements in the object" [2:22]).

Deformation is a terribly important idea and is in fact the key element separating the Anglo-American heritage from that originating on the continent. It appears in the writings of others besides Malevich. It exists, for example, in an even more inchoate state in Ortega y Gasset's *The Dehumanization of Art* than in Malevich's *Essays.* There Ortega makes a case against a transparent art and attempts to explain the new art to some degree: "But to stylize means to deform reality, to derealize; style involves dehumanization."[39] The idea of deformation is present also in the work of Fernand Léger and Alain Robbe-Grillet, though they may not use that specific term, and highly visible in the writing of an American, Morse Peckham, as well as in the criticism of Victor Shklovsky, Malevich's fellow countryman and contemporary. Shklovsky was one of the leading Russian literary formalist critics in that short-lived movement which in its beginning around 1914 was so free to develop but which by 1923 began to be slowed down by party repressions.

Like Fry, Bell, Greenberg and Malevich in the plastic arts and allied to Hulme and the New Critics in literature, Shklovsky and his formalist colleagues react against readings of literature as history, sociology, politics or psychology, and are concerned with what they refer to as the "literariness of literature." But the Russian formalists move beyond the New Critics. The New

Critics variously attempt to posit one or another trope as the basis of all literature, for instance, irony as proposed by Cleanth Brooks. But, as is easily argued, non-poetic language uses tropes as well. Earlier, the Russian formalists found this insufficient.

In his survey essay on the Russian movement, "The Theory of the 'Formal Method,'" Boris Eichenbaum explains how the formalists disposed of both the supremacy of one particular trope, such as the image or symbol, over all others and also "freed themselves from the traditional correlation of 'form and content' and from the traditional idea of form as an envelope, a vessel into which one pours a liquid (the content). The facts of art demonstrate that art's uniqueness consists not in the 'parts' which enter into it but in their original use. Use is key: thus the notion of form was changed: the new notion of form demanded no companion idea, no correlative."[40] The Russian formalists dispense with the form-content dichotomy. They refuse to name one small facet of poetry or fiction as the all-embracing aspect and instead adopt a more general procedure. They classify language as utilitarian or poetic and from this examine language and various devices as the materials which are shaped by motifs into literary structures.[41]

Shklovsky deals with a number of devices or techniques used in the structuring of that remarkable eighteenth-century novel by Laurence Sterne, *The Life and Opinions of Tristram Shandy,*[42] proclaiming in the end that "*Tristram Shandy* is the most typical novel in world literature." Analyzing the difference between story and plot, he attacks the charge that the book is not a novel. According to Shklovksy, story is merely the description of events, raw material to be used in plot construction, and plot need have nothing to do with causality and expectation. *Tristram Shandy* shuns causality while displaying a complex plotting covered with a veneer of apparent chaos. And Shklovsky claims that it is the most typical novel in world literature because of its plot. "The forms of art are explainable by the laws of art; they are not justified by their realism."[43] For Shklovsky transparency and illusion in literature are ploys of naturalism which he associates with story.

Shklovksy employs the term *defamiliarization* in relation to various techniques and devices involved in the construction of works. As a formal element, plot can be used to defamiliarize the story material. Instead of viewing the poem, for example, as a vehicle for condensing, crystallizing and economizing language, or as a means for making the unknown familiar—two traditional positions—he sees it in quite another light. In "Art as Technique" he writes, "And art exists that one may recover the sensation of life; it exists to make one feel things, to make the stone *stony*. The purpose of art is to impart the sensation of things as they are perceived and not as they are known. The technique of art is to make objects 'unfamiliar,' to make forms difficult, to increase the difficulty and length of perception because the process of perception is an aesthetic end in itself and must be prolonged. *Art is a way of experiencing the artfulness of an object; the object is not important.*"[44] This process rids one of automatic perception in which one can no longer see and no longer experience, but only proceed unconsciously by rote.

Shklovsky points out another device related to defamiliarization, one which implies the self-questioning process. As in the case of Sterne the artist may consciously reveal or "lay bare" his techniques so that the perceiver becomes more aware of them than of their pragmatic functions.[45] Of Sterne he writes in this regard: "By violating the form [meaning our assumptions and expectations of the form of the novel] he forces us to attend to it; and for him, this awareness of the form through its violation constitutes the content of the novel."[46]

To defamiliarization and the device of revealing techniques, Shklovsky connects methods of de-automatizing perception—a far cry from Bell's passive aesthetic emotion. Shklovksy's concept of "making strange" or defamiliarizing becomes a decidedly more active tool than the deformation of Malevich. It is disputable and I believe incorrect to assert, as do René Wellek and Austin Warren, that Shklovsky's idea of defamiliarization is one of novelty merely for novelty's sake, and therefore another version of the Romantic Coleridgean or Wordsworthian notions of "making strange."[47] One can refute this in several ways. Shklovksy is dealing not only with the Russian futurist poetry of his day and with the admittedly unique and revolutionary eighteenth-century novel *Tristram Shandy*, but also with other older literary texts and the study of the history of literature. He writes, "The work of art arises from a background of other works and through association with them."[48] Furthermore, his concern with perception arises from a study of techniques used by the artist to break through normative notions of what a novel or poem should be and force the perceiver to examine these works more closely. Shklovksy's interest is not in novelty for its own sake but in "the literariness of literature."

Across the continent in Western Europe the cubists, progenitors of Russian constructivism, were also concerned with questions of form and perception—the how rather than the what. The Russian formalists regarded criticism as a scientific pursuit, that is, they proceeded systematically and analytically to look for literary facts while repudiating the tendency toward impressionistic criticism. Fernand Léger, in his short essay "A New Realism—The Object (Its plastic and cinematic graphic value)" published in 1926 (two years after making the film *Ballet Mécanique* with Dudley Murphy), argues for more systematic and analytic ways of structuring film and our perceptions of film. "All current cinema is romantic, literary, historical, expressionistic, etc.," he wrote polemically. He speaks of "bringing out the values of the object," "the enlarged fragments projected (as a close-up) on the screen," asserting that "in the new realism the human being, the personality, is very interesting only in these fragments and (that) these fragments should not be considered of any more importance than any of the other objects, listed."[49]

Léger argues that use of light, time, rhythm and the isolation of object or person in close-up can restructure film, forcing the viewer to look at it as never before. Léger's cubist film and his essay on cinema are both about deformation and de-automatizing the perception of film, moving it out of a realism in the conventional coded senses. He concludes: "The realism of the cinema is still to be created. It will be the work of the future."

The idea of a new realism includes an abstraction from the representational, as in Léger, as well as the completely nonobjective image, as with Malevich's suprematism. The concept of a new realism (not to be confused with super-realism or with returns to nineteenth-century naturalism) continues in various versions in modernist theory and practice into the second half of this century. In a collection of critical essays by Alain Robbe-Grillet, *For a New Novel: Essays on Fiction,* the new realism of the new novel is implicitly connected with ideas about deformation and discontinuity.

Defending his own novels against charges of anti-humanism by practitioners of socialist realism and Sartrean *engagement,* Robbe-Grillet argues that the work must be perceived in the here and now, and that the writer's only possible commitment is to the act of writing itself. "Each novelist, each novel must invent its own form. No recipe can replace this continual reflection.... Far from respecting certain immutable forms, each new book tends to constitute the laws of its functioning at the same time that it produces their destruction."[50]

Robbe-Grillet was accused of being a "formalist" because of his particular use of description in his novels in which objects and people are given equal value. This practice contradicts traditional humanist values which assert that objects exist to be seen through the anthropomorphosizing eyes of man and for man alone have their raison d'être. With Nathalie Sarraute he suggests that those who use the same outworn forms over and over should be called formalists, not those who see a constant evolution of forms.

Contrasting contemporary with older works, Robbe-Grillet comments on discontinuity and processes of reading: "As much as there was something satisfying in a 'destiny,' even a tragic one, by so much do the finest works of our contemporaries leave us empty, out of countenance. Not only do they claim no other reality than that of the reading, or of the performance, but further they always seem to be in the process of contenting, of jeopardizing themselves in proportion as they create themselves." In the new narrative "space destroys time, and time sabotages space. Description makes no headway, contradicts itself, turns in circles. Moment denies continuity."[51]

By disposing of a humanist value system one is able to let go of old sclerotic forms and invent new ones, vital to one's own times. Just as the world has changed and our conceptions of reality changed with it, "it would scarcely be natural for the foundations of its realism not to have evolved in parallel with these transformations."[52]

The novel is not a mere transcription of reality, a transparency, but constitutes reality, says Robbe-Grillet, through its constantly questioning, changing form.[53] Echoes of Malevich and Shklovsky are strong here. The new realism of Robbe-Grillet's new novel involves the here and now of the reading process in that discontinuous moment, the use of deformation in the description of objects, an anti-humanism and a constant putting into question of form in the construction of the work.

The second line of formalist thinking, though born in Europe, is not exclusively European. Ideas of deformation and discontinuity reappear in the work of a contemporary America, Morse Peckham. Certain issues which Shklovsky implies are brought out more fully in Peckham's *Man's Rage for Chaos* and his *Art and Pornography* without any apparent direct connection to or influence from the Soviet critic's work.

There is a hint of Peckham's major premise in Shklovsky's words: "There is 'order' in art, yet not a single column of a Greek temple stands exactly in its proper order; poetic rhythm is similarly disordered rhythm."[54] In his search for relationships common among the arts, Peckham concerns himself with behaviour, particularly that of the art perceiver. Contrary to the widespread premise that the world is chaos and art in its enduring order represents a respite from that chaos, Peckham uses transactionalism and the expectancy theory of perception to assert the reverse. He holds that one brings to every experience patterns and an orientation, including a set of expectancies, which filter out unnecessary environmental stimuli at the given moment.

Thus the drive in life is one toward order while the perception of art is a relief from this drive.[55] It is through art's form with its discontinuities that one perceives chaos.

Discontinuity, says Peckham, is form's dynamic element. His description of the perceptual act is based on the Leo Postman and Jerome Bruner expectancy or hypothesis theory of perception. According to this three-step theory, the perceptual process involves first an hypothesis or expectancy, then input of information from the environment, and finally a checking or confirmation procedure. If this last is not compatible with the hypothesis an adjustment is made, based on internal personological factors or feedback from the immediately preceding learning experience, in an effort to find a confirmation and reestablish order. Peckham holds then that all perceptual experiences are organized by preexisting patterns in the mind and that in the daily search for order, more categories are added as needed to maintain it.[56]

In applying these notions to art, Peckham seizes upon the first step in this procedure—the expectancy or hypothesis which is brought to every act. For each of the arts expectations are derived from its rules, rules which do not describe but rather prescribe. What they prescribe is not in the work but is instead "a sign for the category the range of which includes as members such expectancies."[57] Peckham presents various examples of definitions on which the perceiver's expectancies of works of art are based. Against these definitions he indicates kinds of discontinuities which come about in actual encounters with works of art. These discontinuities alter one's perception and jolt and disorder one's hypotheses. It is on this premise that he makes form a category residing in the perceiver.

What is significant here is Peckham's stress on the activity of the perceiver and his assertion that nothing is purely objective, so much being conditioned by the perceiver's own background, disposition and orientation. He not only makes the confrontation with the work of art a dynamic one but also disposes of the idea proposed by the New Critics that meaning is somehow anchored and immanent in the work.

It has already been shown how Malevich turns certain fixed terms upside down in grappling with the new arts, maintaining that if *aesthetic* means *beauty,* as it is classically defined, then modern work is neither beautiful nor has anything to do with aesthetics. By breaking through codified assumptions and defying traditional standards, Malevich's tactic opens up new possibilities for work to be considered under the rubric of art. Yet Peckham goes further. In search of relationships among the arts he defines a work of art as "any perceptual field which an

31

individual uses as an occasion for performing the role of art perceiver."[58] Because the term *artifact* is too limiting to include time arts, *perceptual field* is used here and elsewhere the term *stage*.[59] Through culture and learning one possesses clues to a work of art. From the walls of a museum to an orchestral hall to a movie theatre to a comic book to objects on a mantelpiece—there is in each case a stage or setting or perceptual field which is the clue for perceiving it as art.[60] Peckham defines the art perceiver's role as "search-behaviour focussed on awareness of discontinuites."[61]

If one considers this wide range of perceptual fields as art, how then are distinctions made? Peckham returns again to behaviour, perception and discontinuity. He describes culture as a pyramid with art as one of its four sides. The lesser the amount of formal or stylistic discontinuity, the lower the level. More frequent stylistic or formal revolutions occur in art produced at a higher cultural level. For example, one can compare the history of the comic book with that of painting over the last half-century and note the difference in the amount of discontinuity in each and simultaneously the cultural level at which each is aimed. The perceiver, if discontent with the degree of discontinuity at a lower level, will seek an art produced at a higher cultural level.

Peckham does not merely apply his schema to twentieth-century art; in fact his examples are taken largely from the painting, architecture, music and poetry of the seventeenth, eighteenth and early nineteenth centuries. Yet one cannot help recalling here Ortega y Gasset's sociological interest in the unpopularity of the new arts and his prediction that they would never be popular. For Peckham's theory of discontinuities operates particularly well when applied to modernism, the history of the avant-garde and individual works, whether in film or the other arts.

Peckham's concern with discontinuity and expectation can be related to earlier theories. But one sees in Peckham a more active, conscious, almost aggressive sense of the perceiver's role in the art encounter. This emphasis raises an inevitable question: Is Peckham reasserting the form-content dichotomy? One can argue that he is not, or if he is then not in the manner of a socialist realist or a Kracauer-styled humanist. For instance, Peckham is not concerned with art as it relates to sociology or psychology and accepts the fact that art's semantic aspect is equally obtainable from other areas of culture. In a sense, by positing form as a transaction based on the expectancies established through patterns of behaviour, prescriptive definitions of art and other prior learning experiences, Peckham still in fact leaves the work intact.

It simply is and needs no justification for its existence—or should need none. The issue is one's ability to approach and perceive the object and what it, as art, does for one. Peckham's answer is that stylistic discontinuities fulfill "man's rage for chaos." But despite the active perceptual apparatus offered by his theory, he seems almost to reduce art to the biological and physiological levels.

The *real* and a *new realism* are both terms used by Malevich, Léger and other cubists, Robbe-Grillet, members of de Stijl, futurists and constructivists, as well as Fry and Bell— in a word by practitioners of both kinds of formalism. Whatever the area of greatest interest, there is in each a concern with the work of art in itself. The same is true of others such as Shklovsky or Peckham who might not explicitly use these terms. By attending to the art at hand, each hopes to dispose of criticism that deals with the critic's own quirks or with biography, literary history or psychology, the work itself considered merely a symptom of the artist's or of the period's problems. In so doing the Russian formalists thought of the critical practice as a scientific one, while Greenberg saw the enclosure, the self-criticism, the justification of a work by itself as a cultural activity analogous to and made possible by the workings of pure science.

"I do not transcribe, I construct," writes Robbe-Grillet.[62] The importance of these concepts of a new realism, the object in itself or the literariness of literature is that art is not seen as a naturalistic, intact, automatic transposition from life. Art is made, is separate, is meant to be scrutinized and felt. It is full of fissures, deformations and discontinuities—elements with which in one way or another the formalists of the second group are concerned. It is deformation which is the key to evaluating the two directions of formalism.

While Greenberg can evoke science for the cause of modernism, the New Critics shrink from it. But in the end there is little difference between them. Fry, Bell, the New Critics and Greenberg fall back on traditional notions—taste, aesthetic emotion, inspiration, value—for some kind of continuity with the past as well as for a means of separating the realm of the aesthetic from the utilitarian. Their more conservative version of formalism eliminates many formal possibilities and new directions, retreating into a cul de sac, ossifying itself. Its methods disguise a traditional position, while the other direction from Malevich through Robbe-Grillet and Peckham makes possible a questioning of artistic and cultural values and leads itself, in a sense, out of itself.

The break-up of modernism during the minimalist phase is a

history of the effects of one kind of formalism in theory and practice. In the visual arts, especially in the United States in the early 1960s, Greenberg's ideas exerted an extraordinary influence. Robbe-Grillet's essays dating from the early fifties to the early sixties were only published in the United States in translation in a collected anthology in 1965. The ideas of the Russian formalists were not widely known, especially in visual arts circles in the sixties, and Malevich hadn't yet had his renaissance. So it was the formalist ideas of Greenberg, the background of abstract expressionism followed by post-painterly abstraction and certain activities in sculpture which created the ambience for the emergence of minimal art.

Minimalism in the mid-sixties pushed the question of the object to its limits. Minimal art was characterized in part by the use of exact repetition in serial works, non-hierarchial and holistic structures, industrial materials manufactured to specification, a repudiation of all metaphor and symbol, and at that time, claims of a neutral art in a neutral context, i.e., a value-free art. The minimal work is self-contained, distanced, challenging the viewer reflexively to engage with it. It is a highly intellectualized art about form; it is a hyperbolization of the idea of the object, concrete yet abstract, anti-illusionistic and factual. Minimalist painting by Robert Ryman and Robert Mangold and sculpture by Donald Judd and Carl Andre represents the limits of that emphasis on the object, on self-containment, on form, on the abstract-concrete. Process art as practiced by Eva Hesse, Robert Morris and others reacted against minimalism, taking exception to the idea of the object and to self-containment. It valued the incompleteness of the work and the procedures used in making it as much or more than the final product. Sol LeWitt, falling somewhere between minimal and conceptual art, claimed that all art is about ideas and it is the ideas that count, working out certain geometric givens in sculpture and in wall drawings with accompanying texts and books of drawings. Like the conceptualists he wanted to de-emphasize form in search of other definitions of art. Conceptual art was part of the Duchampian heritage that reacted against the Anglo-American formalism of Clive Bell, Roger Fry and Clement Greenberg and led to a postmodernism.

It is unfortunate that the differences between the two kinds of formalism are ignored. One can see how the conservative Anglo-American direction, tradition-bound with its notions of taste, inspiration, artisanry and value can lead to a tautology and a hermeticism. That minimal art went beyond this critical conception of form in part by literalizing the works of art which were its products is culturally and socially important.

The other strand of formalism uses its principles of deformation, discontinuity and defamiliarization in order to break with old ideas. One could suggest that in fact it bears the seeds of its auto-destruction through these same principles.

What is important in both kinds of formalism is the consideration of the work of art as art—a position which has been the object of a great deal of criticism along the lines of "art for art's sake." The technical description of a work of art according to criteria of quality and good taste is a formalism at its worst. But the act of treating that work as a construction in the world rather than an imitation or an emotional encoding of it is crucial. The realism of the present event, the discontinuous moment of encounter with the work is significant. That certain recent art such as conceptual or earlier body or process art defies the holistic aspect of an object does not vitiate the entire direction of the second kind of formalism. A close reading of a work of art does not eliminate other readings—social, biographical, political—but it should precede these others.

Where is Michael Snow in all of this? Of the critics and artists discussed in terms of formalism, none mention photography and only one, Léger, treats film. One can better understand Snow's work by examining the critical and artistic directions of formalism in modernism than by looking to the ideas of Bazin, Kracauer, Panofsky or Cavell. Snow can use the automatism of the camera to construct with it, to destroy certain assumptions about the work, or to de-automatize the process of perception for the viewer.

Snow began concentrating on camera-related art while minimalism was on the rise and modernism put into question, especially that part of modernism in the visual arts connected with a reductivism. Against the background just presented which stresses the importance of formalist thinking in relation to modern art, I wish now to figure in Snow, locating his art within the second tradition of formalism which, as shall be seen, finally moves beyond itself in its constant self-questioning.

Chapter 3

Photographic Objects

In 1967 Snow's career began turning significantly in the direction of camera-related art with the completion of *Wavelength,* photographic works and camera-influenced sculpture. One of the sculptures is *Portrait,* an aluminum frame of variable dimensions which can be stretched or contracted to wedge in between walls. The window is there; the framing will change, depending upon each particular installation and upon the viewer's position. *Portrait* operates from both sides; it frames the viewer at the same time that it frames the gallery space the viewer sees.

The word *portrait* makes one think more of pictorial or verbal manifestations than of sculptural ones. A portrait, as a work of art, is representational. Here *Portrait,* perhaps oxymoronically, is both object and presentation, always with the potential to change at the viewer's will. As in a portrait the perceiver is framed and presented for spectators on the other side. But the viewer can never see his or her self-portrait. Snow's *Portrait* is always a presentation, never a representation. Here is an example of Peckham's idea about extending the stage for art. The work plays, especially through its title, on presentational versus representational and on the real and the art object. Snow's *Portrait* presents only itself and a heightened awareness of its surroundings as they appear within its borders.

Portrait is a touchstone to the photographs. And Snow's photographs, in turn, have much in common with his films, although they might not seem to at first glance. Snow can take representational materials, here photographic materials, which document or give information and make autonomous objects of them. *Portrait* frames; the photographic works frame in particular ways. Snow's "portrait" is about itself; his photographic objects are often about themselves and nearly always use representational rather than abstract images.

Snow's use of photography is idiosyncratic and anomalous. Almost all of Snow's photographic works include more than one image, whether in series or serial, or in superimposition. I use the term *photographic works* because it includes photographic prints, 35mm slides and Polaroids and quite often so-called mixed media, in which the photographs are prime or share a prime place. *A Casing Shelved* has an audiotape with its 35mm slide or its photographic print; *Glares* and *Light Blues* each have a lamp included; *Authorization* has a mirror, and so on. Others

6. *Portrait*
Photo: Isaacs Gallery

have special mounting devices. Many of these are unique because in the final work something employed in the process of making the photograph—mirror, light, etc.—is included. Others are in limited editions. In this chapter I will focus on those photographic works which emphasize the object; the slide pieces and the photographic book, *Cover to Cover,* which lead to other issues will be discussed later.

Snow's use of photography defies both the traditional notion of the nature of the medium as a simple documentary process which mirrors the world, and the stance represented by Walter Benjamin, who sees the reproduced image as changing art and attitudes toward art by way of providing more and greater access to works of art themselves. Snow's photographic works do something else entirely, whether as prints alone or incorporated in mixed media.

37

7. *Midnight Blue*
Photo: Isaacs Gallery

Framing is a key to the object aspect in Snow's work. This is evident in *Midnight Blue* of 1973-74 (wood, acrylic, colour photograph and wax, 28¾" x 26"). Snow photographed a candle against a painted blue wood backboard, the candle providing the only illumination. The backboard is constructed of rough planks running horizontally. The life-size photograph is applied in position against the backboard. It is framed top and sides by a strip of lighter blue, what was not captured by the camera when filmed under low illumination, which now contrasts with the dark blue of the photograph. Both are framed by the remaining unpainted wood. On the bottom is a ledge containing candle wax, traces from the burning candle when it was photographed. Cutting through from the corners of the unpainted wood are diagonal lines which intersect at the centre of the dark blue photograph. There is another diagonal cut into the ledge crossing at the point where the candle had been placed when photographed. *Midnight Blue* becomes a kind of intellectual trompe-l'oeil in which Snow mixes illusion with evidences of the real. From across the room the eye can be deceived by the candle, but on inspection one adjusts and places it in its space; the X cutting across the photograph above the image of the candle flattens the space, eliminating the illusion of depth beyond the candle.

Snow undermines the nature of the photograph, its realism, by playing on the convincing and deceptive nature of that illusion. But it is not about a super-realism. The careful framing brings together the original event with its representation, reframing the representation to correspond with remnants of the real—the wax drippings. We can be deceived but are then immediately undeceived. There are traces of both the illusory and the real—a play on the transfer of reality, on the indexical properties of film.

In three other works these indexical aspects, carefully framed, are emphasized more specifically: *Field* (1973-74), *Crouch, Leap, Land* (1970) and *Press* (1969). Of the three, two are unique while there is an edition of three of *Crouch, Leap, Land*.

Field (70½" x 66¾") consists of 101 images. Snow scattered emulsified paper in a field to produce photograms of leaves, grass, etc.; ninety-eight of these mirror one another in positive and negative (one has no corresponding image). Below are two large photographs, one positive and one negative, of the field with its photographic paper in the process of registering images. *Field* contains the microscopic and the macroscopic. What at first looks abstract, without order, is in fact concrete and immediate and also quite ordered. The photogram displays most completely and directly the indexical properties of film. One can see the

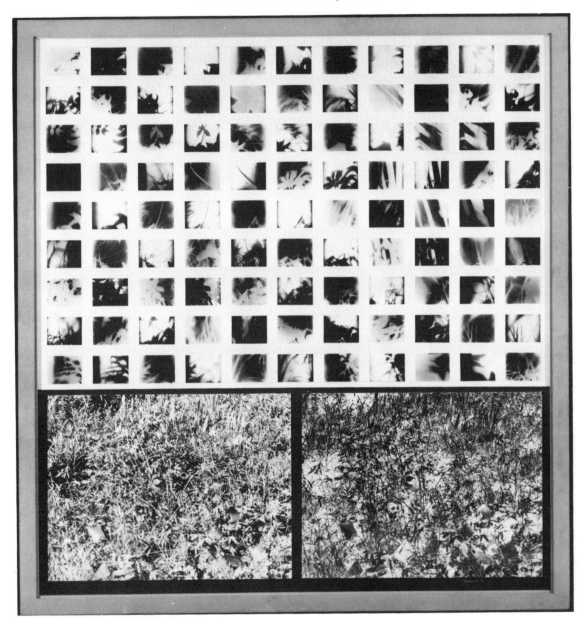

8. *Field*
Photo: The National Gallery of Canada

process of recording reflected twice over—through the mirroring in positive and negative and through the large images of the small pieces of photographic paper at the time of their being activated by light in the field.

The series and the two large prints cover opposite image qualities and simultaneous time. In this way the work falls back on itself. *Field* is about the registration and ordering of the images rather than about the field itself, which is dissected and analyzed for the process.

39

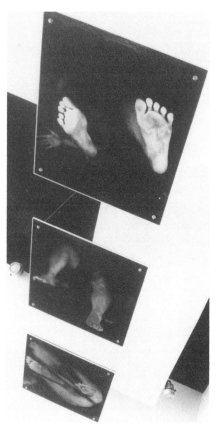

9. *Crouch, Leap, Land*
Photo: Michael Snow

If *Field* recalls Man Ray and his rayograms and Moholy-Nagy and his photograms, one might think with some humour about Muybridge in conjunction with *Crouch, Leap, Land*. It consists of three black-and-white photographic prints, each 24" x 24". Each is mounted under plexiglass and suspended from the ceiling, hung low, image facing the floor. Its title literally describes the event. "The image of a woman is seen pressed against the picture plane, leaving it, and landing on it. It is the reconstruction of three phases of an action (a woman jumping from and landing back on a piece of clear plexiglass, under which a camera is placed...."[1] It is voyeuristic. The viewer must crouch down and look up at the woman's image, physically assuming a position like the one taken by the cameraman while shooting. *Crouch, Leap, Land* in this way anticipates a later film work, *Two Sides to Every Story,* in which the viewing situation is isomorphic with its making. It is as if in some way, in illusion, the woman were pressing on the camera through the plexiglass, impressing her image on it. As voyeurism always has more to do with the subject than the object, this work reflects back on the viewers, their responses, their awarenesses of the enclosure of the event. The manner of framing serves the voyeuristic illusion; at the same time the self-consciousness of the framing and viewing situation calls attention back to the work itself.

In *Press* (72¾" x 72" x 10¼", 16 black-and-white photographic prints, plexiglass and metal clamps), Snow literalizes and puns through his title. Objects were pressed between plexiglass and polished metal and photographed. The emphatic distortion resulting from this procedure is a parodistic reinforcement of the two-dimensionality of photography. Snow carries this idea further by re-pressing all sixteen photographs under plexiglass and securing them with clamps. Pressing becomes equivalent to framing in which the objects are distorted as if frozen out of shape. The framing stamps the index; the framing makes the index in this case.

Besides the emphasis on the indexical properties of photography, the aspect of process is unescapable in the four works just described. And process is connected with both framing and the object. The idea of object and process coming together seems a contradiction. One thinks about objects in space and processes in time. The two can coexist, of course, in the time-space medium of film, but a photographic work is marked out, delineated by a frame and defined as a spatial art, not a temporal one.

In characterizing Snow's 1969 work *Authorization,* Brydon Smith uses the phrase "realism of process,"[2] recalling Robert Fulford's comments quoted earlier about Snow's art being about

40

10. *Press*
Photo: Ayriss, Isaacs Gallery

a "special kind of realism, based not on something outside art but rather on the very nature of the art-act itself and on the nature of 'reality' as experienced and as depicted." Perhaps *Authorization* (Polaroids, mirror, frame, 30" x 20") is one of the best examples, perhaps the best example of his unique photographic objects.

41

11. *Authorization*. The reflections in the mirror have been inappropriately masked out.
Photo: The National Gallery of Canada

Snow taped off a rectangle in the centre of a mirror the measure of four Polaroid prints. Focusing on the mirror image of himself within the taped area, he took one Polaroid shot, glued it to the upper left of the taped rectangle, snapped another, secured it to the upper right, finally completing the rectangle with two more stills. He then took the fifth and last shot which he placed in the upper left-hand corner of the frame of the mirror.

Authorization self-describes and one recognizes the puns involved in the title as Snow authorizes his own image. The entire process is clear, laid out, can be traced by any viewer proceeding forward from the first to the fifth Polaroid or backward from the last to the first. It demystifies the idea of the author by revealing the steps of its procedure of reproduction, yet it still makes an object, and a unique object, which can be repeated by retracing the steps, remaking the work, which only Snow can authorize.

Red^5 and *Morning in Holland* are closely related to *Authorization* in terms of process. In *Red^5* of 1974 (photographic dye transfer print, 25" x 31"), a red field was photographed and rephotographed, each succeeding Polaroid placed on the field so that it appears in the next shot, until finally there are four included in the fifth and final photograph. While it is close to *Authorization* in terms of process and also in framing, it must be noted that it doesn't exist as object as do *Authorization* and *Morning in Holland:* it has no elements incorporated into its final form as does *Authorization* nor is it a unique object as are the two other works.

Morning in Holland (colour photographs, tape, paper and enamel, 49" x 48") was made over a five-year period from 1969 to 1974. Snow has commented that instead of being added to as is the case with *Authorization* and *Red^5*, it is a curiously subtractive work. At the same time it is one whose process is much more difficult to recreate in the perceiver's time and also more difficult to describe. On a white surface Snow taped sixteen rectangular frames, four in each of four colours—red, yellow, blue and green—each colour arranged in a different position in the four rows. He then covered the whole with black paper, positioned his tripoded camera in front and proceeded to cut away the black paper one frame and one colour at a time, photographing each step until all frames were exposed and the entire rectangle emptied of black. Each of the sixteen photographs was then placed in its corresponding square, marking the unmasking of that colour. Finally, then, the entire asymmetrical process can be retraced.

Morning in Holland, about colour, light and its absence, can be characterized as abstract. But at the same time because of the

43

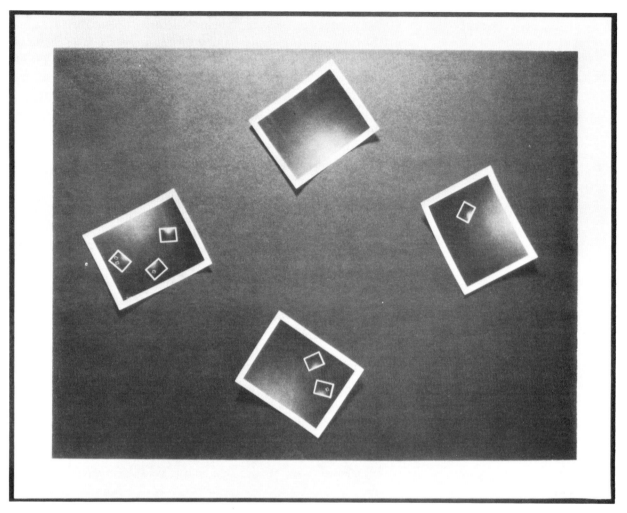

12. *Red*[5]
Photo: The National Gallery of Canada

13. Above right, *Morning in Holland*
Photo: Isaacs Gallery

14. Below right, *A Wooden Look*
Photo: The National Gallery of Canada

process of its creation it is representational of the traces of that process. The title is a clear reference to Mondrian and even to de Stijl—both of which again suggest particular idiosyncratic ideas of realism as they appear in various modern movements. One also thinks of Malevich and his notions of a nonobjective art. As in many of Snow's other photographic works, time is so clearly traced in space; one could indeed say that time here is representational.

There is another kind of abstraction apparent in *Glares* (1973), *A Wooden Look* (1969) and *Of a Ladder* (1971). Each makes use of a kind of camera distortion called optical bend. From its stationary tripod position the camera changes only its shooting angle as it films up and down and/or across a large or a long object, thereby registering degrees of visual warp or bend. In the two ladder works the camera records distortions along their lengths. The process involved in *Glares* (58¾" x 39½") is more difficult to retrace but one is assisted by the hanging lamp which is

44

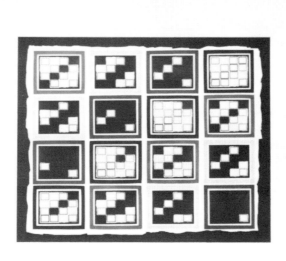

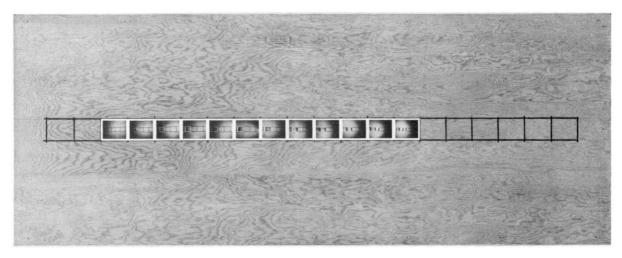

45

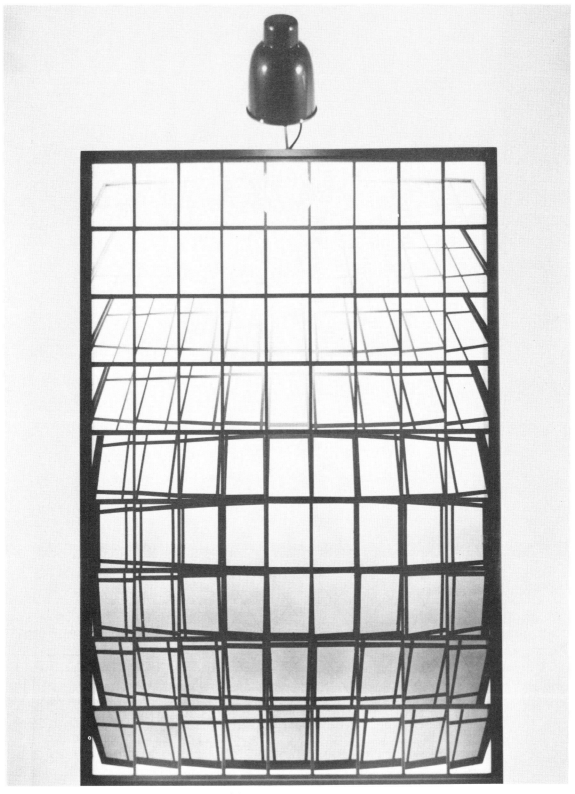

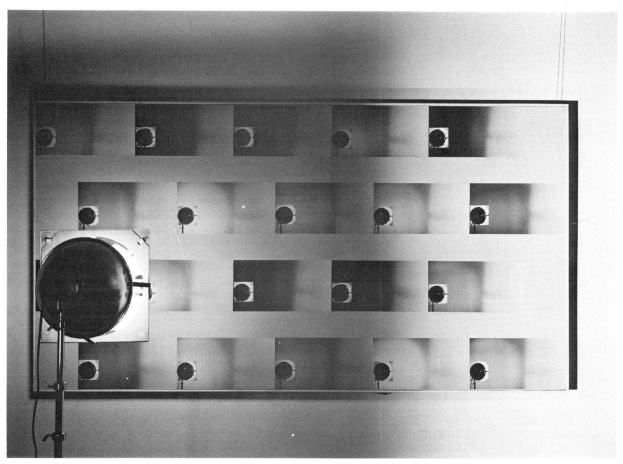

15. Left, *Glares*
Photo: T.E. Moore, Isaacs Gallery

16. Above, *Light Blues*
Photo: Isaacs Gallery

included at the top, the one actually used in the shooting of the photographs. *Glares* contains ninety-nine photographs as well as its lamp. As all ninety-nine grids were filmed from the same tripod position, the photographs on top are much lighter than the bottom ones and all are distorted by optical bend. The lamp is a doubling device, doubling or repeating the procedure by casting the same amount of illumination in the final construction as it had cast in the photographic process.

Light Blues of 1974 (colour photographic prints and lamp, 38" x 72") is also an object which uses doubling and word play. It is made with coloured light. There are ten photographs, each printed twice, arranged in four rows of five each and mounted on a white surface. A standing lamp covered with a blue filter is placed at the left side and casts its light over the left half of the piece. Each of the twenty photographs is an image of that same lamp, to the left side of the frame, covered with one of ten different coloured filters and projecting that colour against a background. The blue filter from the actual standing lamp changes the colour fields. The presentation and the representation exist here together. The work is objectified through the framing and the doubling presence of the lamp.

In *Light Blues* the photographic process is clear and repeated over and over, with only a change in coloured light. In some ways it is related to an earlier work of 1966-67, *Atlantic* (photographic prints and tinned metal sheets, 70" x 96" x 12"). In this piece thirty photographs of ocean waves are housed individually in twelve-inch-deep metal boxes. The images are reflected in the metal and even seem to reverberate. These photographs were taken at the same time that the photograph of waves was made for the film *Wavelength*. *Atlantic* breaks up the illusion of depth at the same time that it plays with it intensely, with its highly reflective frames making the waves appear to float back and forth. These extremely seductive images are also quite abstract as each is flat and continuous, bearing no horizon line. This two-fold aspect—the representational combined with the abstract/concrete—is characteristic of much of Snow's work. Unlike *Glares* and *Light Blues, Atlantic* is not about process, but like *Light Blues* it uses repetition of the same or a closely related image to objectify the work.

Objects incorporated into works are used to double, to refer back to and to clarify the process of making, finally to objectify the working process itself. That is the case with the lamps in *Light Blues* and *Glares,* and the inseparable mirror in *Authorization. Log* of 1973-74 (colour photograph, plexiglass and log; log—110¼" x 26" x 9¼", photo—56¾" x 9¼")is another literal work, but unlike *Field* or the punning *Press* it does not merely describe and reframe the acts of making, nor does it simply describe and double the event like *Crouch, Leap, Land.* An actual log exists alongside its photographic representation. One might recall Joseph Kosuth's earlier works such as *One and Three Chairs* of 1965 in which he uses a real chair, a photograph of it and a dictionary definition of *chair.* This was part of Kosuth's preoccupation at that time—very early in the development of conceptual art—with definitions of art and with changing those definitions, breaking out of a sealed circle whose parameters were either postpainterly abstraction or minimalism. While these two movements were quite different in terms of Greenbergian formalist definitions, for Kosuth and other conceptual artists they were related by their limitations.

One and Three Chairs is a didactic work attempting to use art to present philosophical ideas, some of which are involved with examining and changing definitions of art. For Kosuth, the idea and the intention matter more than the object per se or than the purely perceptual act; in this way he attempts to break down a certain kind of formal hegemony. But in Snow's *Log,* made nine years later, the terms and interests are different. For him the object is indeed important. The thing becomes an object as well as the subject of representation. Here there is both presentation and representation. Neither framing nor process are of importance in this work, whereas doubling and literalization are, as well as the obvious comment on the real and the illusory. The three-dimensional log casts its shadow, which of course the reduced and reproduced flat image of it cannot do.

Tap (1969), of which a photograph is one of its five elements, returns again to framing along with references to conceptual art. A second element is a text in which Snow lists all five parts: "I wanted to make a composition which was dispersed, in which the elements would be come upon in different ways and which would consist of 1. a sound, 2. an image, 3. a text, 4. an object, and 5. a line [of wire], which would be unified but the parts of which would be of interest in themselves if the connections between them were not seen (but better if seen)."[3] *Tap* names what is heard, while the photograph represents how the sound is made as it is being heard: one of Snow's hands holds a microphone while the fingers of the other hand lightly tap on the instrument. The object seen is a brown speaker. The text describes the gathering of materials, costs, decisions, intentions and relationships of parts. "Since the brown speaker frames the sound, I used the same brown in framing both this (the text) and the photo."[4]

Whether or not intentionally, *Tap* recalls certain preoccupations of conceptual art. Characterizing the line of wire as an "object" recalls conceptual art's antithetical concern with the dematerialization of art. *Tap* becomes almost a parody of framing in which the speaker frames the sound, the brown colour of the speaker is used on frames for the image and the text, and the image is one of hands framed on a tape recorder making sound. Once again as in Snow's other photographic works the references are internal, falling back on themselves.

Quite unlike *Tap* or *Log* is a work of 1976, *Imposition* (colour photograph, 72" x 40"). Other than his book, *Cover to Cover,* this is his only photographic work to use superimposition. Four photographs—picturing a wall and floor, a couch, a couple clothed, and the same couple nude—are superimposed, slightly off registration. The molding of the room lightly floats on the couch as a ghost image; the couple's naked bodies as if in X-ray are faintly visible through their clothing. The photograph is hung on its side so that the horizon line is perpendicular to the floor. The couple is looking, their heads craned to one side, at what

49

17. *Tap.* Part Three, text.
Photo: The National Gallery of Canada

18. Right, *Imposition*
Photo: Michael Snow

TAP (PART THREE)

THE "DRUMMING" SOUND WHICH YOU HAVE HEARD, ARE HEARING, WILL HEAR OR PERHAPS WONT EVER HEAR I MADE BY TAPPING MY FINGERS AGAINST A MICROPHONE WHILE MOVING IT OVER THE TAPE RECORDER TO MAKE A BIT OF FEEDBACK. I THEN MADE A LOOP OF A SELECTION FROM THE RESULTING TAPE. THERE IS A LARGE BLOWUP OF A PHOTOGRAPH OF THE ABOVE PROCEDURE WHICH YOU MAY HAVE SEN OR WILL SEE ETC. ITS SUPPOSED TO BE HANGING SOMEWHERE IN THIS BUILDING. THE TAPE AND THE PHOTO WERE MADE IN FEBRUARY 1969 AND THIS IS BEING TIPED ON MARCH 14 1969. JOYCE WIELAND SNOW AND I TOOK THE PHOTOS WITH A MIRANDA 35MM. CAMERA, AN 8"x10" PRINT FROM THE SELECTED NEGATIVE WAS MADE BY "MODERNAGE" ON 48TH STREET AND THE 6' X40" BLOWUP WAS MADE BY "INDEPENDANT" ON 42ND STREET. IT COST $36.00.

I WANTED TO MAKE A COMPOSITION WHICH WAS DISPERSED, IN WHICH THE ELEMENTS WOULD BE BE COME UPON IN DIFFERENT WAYS AND WHICH WOULD CONSIST OF 1. A SOUND, 2. AN IMAGE, 3. A TEXT, 4. AN OBJECT, 5. A LINE, WHICH WOULD BE UNIFIED BUT THE PARTS OF WHICH WOULD BE OF INTEREST IN THEMSELVES IF THE CONNECTIONS BETWEEN THEM WERE NOT SEEN (BUT BETTER IF SEEN). ONE OF MANY ADDITIONAL CONSID ERATIONS WAS THAT IT BE PARTLY TACTILE, BODY MADE THO USING MACHINES. TYPEWRITING IS A VERY SIMILAR FINGER TAPPING TO THE WAY THE TAPE WAS MADE AND I THOUGHT THAT PERHAPS I SHOULD MAKE A COMPLEMENTARY OBJECT BY FINGER TAPPING BUT FINALLY DECID ED TO SHOW THE LOUDSPEAKER AS THE OBJECT, AS A "FOUND" ELEMENT WHICH SPREADS THE "CREATED" ELEMENT. THE SPEAKER IS JUST A CHEAP PORTABLE SPEAKER I GOT ABOUT FIVE YEARS AGO AND I CONSIDERED "INCLUDING" IT MORE BY PAINTING IT, PERHAPS I WILL, AT THIS WRITING IT IS DARK BROWN, ITS ORIGINAL COLOR. RATHER THAN CHANGE THE "GIVEN" COLOR OF THE SPEAKER OR ITS SHAPE I DECIDED TO CONTINUE THE COLOR. THIS AND THE PHOTO ARE BLACK AND WHITE AND THE WIRE IS BLACK. SINCE THE BROWN SPEAKER "FRAMES" THE SOUND I USED THE SAME BROWN IN FRAMING BOTH THIS AND THE PHOTO. THE FRAMES ARE ALSO RECTANGULAR "LOOPS". THE LINE, WHICH OF COURSE, PROPERLY SPEAKING IS ALSO AN OBJECT I DECIDED TO COMPOSE THROUGH WHATEVER BUILDING THE PIECE IS IN. IT PARTLY "COMPOSES" ITSELF ACCORDING TO ITS OWN NATURE BUT IT EVENTUALLY "DISAPPEARS" TO THE TAPE RECORDER WHICH IS NOW(?) PLAYING THE TAPE SO THAT IT (THE WIRE) HAS A "SPREAD" WHICH IN ITS OWN TERMS HAS SOME SIMILARITY TO THE ACOUSTICAL SPACIAL SPREAD OF THE SOUND, EVENTUALLY DISAPPEARING. I DECIDED AGAINST SHOWING THE PLAYBACK TAPE RECORDER BECAUSE THE SOURCE OF THE SOUND AT THIS TIME AND HISTORICALLY IS HERE DESCRIBED AND IN THE PHOTO, PICTURED. IN A SENSE THE BLA CK LINE (CARRIER OF THE SOUND) DISAPPEARS TO HERE (TEXT) TO THE PHOTOGRAPH (IMAG E) BOTH OF WHICH ARE "TRACES" OF IT AND TO THE ACTUAL (HIDDEN) TAPE RECORDER.

THIS PIECE IS AN ATTEMPT TO, AMONG OTHER THINGS, DO SOMETHING MANIPUL ATIVE WITH MEMORY DEVICES: TAPE RECORDER, CAMERA, TYPEWRITER. IT IS NOT A "MIXED MEDIA" OR COLLAGE ASSEMBLAGE PIECE, NOR IS IT THEATRE. AS IS PROPER TO THE USE OF THE ABOVE DEVICES IVE ATTEMPTED TO USE MEMORY AS AN ASPECT OF THE WORK. I HAVE MADE SEPARATED OR "DISPERSED" COMPOSITIONS SINCE 1961, SOME OF THEM HAVING PARTS ON DIFFERENT CONTINENTS BUT WITH THE EXCEPTION OF CERTAIN PERFORMANCE PIECES (EG. "RIGHT READER" 1965) AND FILMS (SIMULTANEOUS IN ELEMENTS AND SITE) THE PARTS WERE ALWAYS IN THE SAME MEDIUM, INVOLVED, IMAGES ONLY (IF THATS POSS IBLE) OR WORKED IN AN IMAGE TO OBJECT SCALE.

"TAP" IS A KIND OF STILL SOUND MOVIE. THE WAYS IN WHICH THE DIFFERE NT ELEMENTS OCCUPY SPACE ARE INTERESTING: THE SOUND FILLING IT, HAVING A SOURCE BUT NO DEFINITE "EDGES", THE LINE, READING BACKWARDS, THREADING AND CARRYING THE SOUND AND HAVING AN UNSEEN END, THE IMAGE FLAT, TWO DIMENSIONAL, THIS FLAT, BLACK, LINEAR, SMALL, IN YOUR EYES AND IN YOUR MIND.

Michael Snow

MICHAEL SNOW

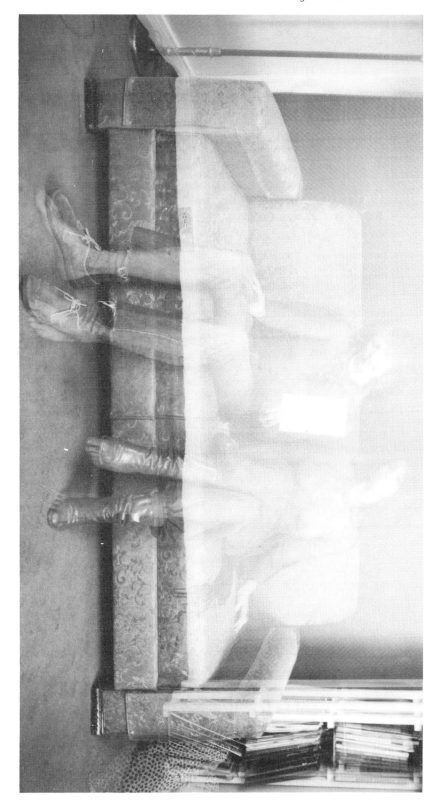

appears to be a white rectangle the man is holding upright in his hand.

With its diaphanous superimposition and sensuous colour the image is quite extraordinary, while the hanging of the photograph is a puzzle. *Imposition* seems at first completely different from Snow's other photographic works. But is it?

This is not the first time that unusual activity is required of the viewer in order to take in one of Snow's works. This element has already been pointed out in connection with *Crouch, Leap, Land* and will be seen again later in *Two Sides to Every Story*. But this is more puzzling, for the viewers must bend their necks to observe what the couple is craning to examine. Unlike *Crouch, Leap, Land* in which viewers are forced to duplicate the process of making in the course of observing, *Imposition* forces them to duplicate what the couple in the photograph is doing. Is the white rectangle, as has been suggested, a photograph of themselves?[5] A likely inference is that the couple is looking at the same photograph the viewers see and taking up the same position they must to read it. Thus *Imposition* is still about the process, but the process of perceiving rather than making.

Many of Snow's favourite themes recur—literally multiplied and/or enlarged—in five very recent works. One, *Plus Tard,* was made in 1977 for the exhibition which toured France in 1977-78, entitled "Michael Snow: Sept films et *Plus Tard*." It appeared with the other four which were executed specifically for Snow's major traveling exhibition of films, photographic works and sculpture which opened in Paris at Centre Georges Pompidou in late 1978. Of these, three are of particular interest: *Multiplication Table, Plus Tard* and *Painting*.

Multiplication Table (43" x 74") is an enormously enlarged photograph of a sketch for a table, executed on a rough-hewn table with a pencil shown completing the table's dimensions which read 32" by 45" by 28" high. The blow-up is mounted low on the wall, in fact extends a few inches out onto the gallery floor. In the enlarged photograph the sketched table, at least in the dimensions of its height and length, approximates its planned size once built. The rough wooden surface on which the drawing lies while being completed alludes to the finished table, and the pencil looms large and out of proportion to the drawn table, thereby confusing the scale of illusions. The enormous close-up of the wooden table's surface exaggerates its texture: what was a small drawing for a table now approaches the proportions of its finished object, and a pencil whose literally overshadowing presence enters from the right casts more doubts on the eye-deceiving illusions.

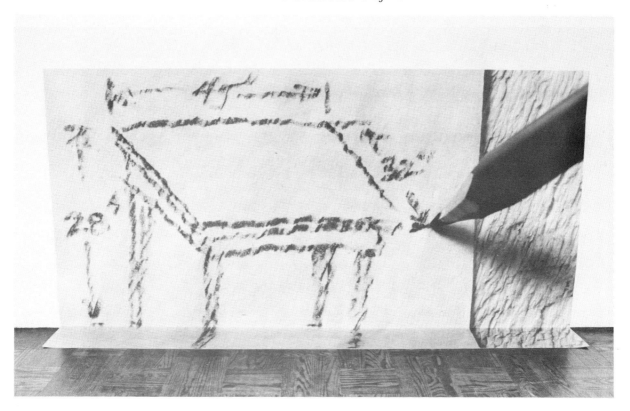

19. *Multiplication Table*
Photo: T.E. Moore, Isaacs Gallery

20-26. Following four pages, *Plus Tard*
Photos: The National Gallery of Canada

With its punning title, *Multiplication Table* is almost a photographic relief. It is without an external frame, yet it is certainly set off. Its conscious scalar confusions play with the old philosophical dichotomies between truth and illusion, reality and appearance, using the perennial classroom example of the real and the ideal table. In his earlier *"Rameau's Nephew"*. . . (see chapter 8) Snow comically jests with these philosophical questions over an appearing and disappearing table. Though they may be disguised in jest and punning, these are issues which continue seriously through Snow's work.

Multiplication Table quite actively engages the viewer by its disconcerting placement and size and its play with layers of depth against flatness. One must walk around to take it in. *Plus Tard* and *Painting* also elicit active viewer participation. *Plus Tard* consists of a sequence of twenty-five colour photographs of varying sizes although each is enclosed in a black frame of the same size (33⅞" x 42½"). The photographs are sandwiched between two sheets of plexiglass so that more or less of the gallery wall with some of the shadow is revealed in the space between the photographs and the frame's inner edge (except for those photographs which fill the entire area to the frame). Snow shot the photographs in a room housing a collection of the Group of

Seven at the National Gallery of Canada. The print sizes vary according to the camera's distance from each object in the course of shooting.

In making *Plus Tard* Snow photographed around the room so that occasionally one sees exit signs and doors. A painting as shot may be exactly in focus with its photograph filling the frame. Or as Snow passed with his camera he might blur the same painting or the following one or frame only half of a work. Also, parts of two paintings might be framed in one image, or with time exposure shooting in a long shot taken at an angle several paintings and the light source in the room will be streaked or smeared in the frame or the images will be multiplied out of focus. At other times a painting is abstracted into an extremely soft focus. The colours of the paintings are changed radically in the photographs, contingent on shooting speed, lighting and other variables.

The very title *Plus Tard* suggests a list of associations—time, delay, return to, memory, recall—in questions of artistic representation and presentation. A landscape painting is a representation. A photograph of it is a representation of a representation. Whether exactly focussed or blurred and abstracted, the photograph is still a representation of the painting in a new presentation, a new form. But now (or rather later) in the photographs in

Plus Tard the paintings cease to be the subject. They are material for a new work, as is the case in *One Second in Montreal* and in *Side Seat Paintings Slides Sound Film* of 1970 in which Snow used slides of his paintings going back to the fifties.

When the photos in *Plus Tard* are arranged over the four walls of a room, as Snow prefers to have them viewed, the sequence recalls in fragments the other space where the actual paintings were hung, while at the same time the new presentation and representations are foregrounded. The history of the paintings takes on a new history in another medium with the traces of photographic time in the sequencing of a new work, *Plus Tard*.

Painterly references sometimes come up in Snow's photographic work. In the early history of photography, artists such as Henry Peach Robinson and Oscar Gustave Rejlander attempted to recreate painting through composite prints. Photographers often used the still life and other painting themes rife with art historical allusions in their work. These were tactics to endow photography with the aura of acceptability then attached to the fine art of painting. But Snow uses painterly references in a totally different way. As mentioned earlier, *Morning in Holland* has its allusions to de Stijl and Mondrian. In *Midnight Blue* Snow plays with the still life and trompe l'oeil. In *Plus Tard* he uses paintings themselves. Significantly, a recent work, a composite of something like 300 photographs in the final print, is called *Painting (Closing the Drum Book)*.[6] It is placed on a low pedestal, at a slight angle to the floor. The images are colour fields, as is the case with *Morning in Holland*, rather than representations, as with *Plus Tard*.

In this extraordinary work so many of Snow's preoccupations and working procedures come together: framing, distortion, the repetition of processes, abstraction and a continued interest in painting. In making *Painting* Snow used one large red ground. On it he placed sixteen other painted rectangles which were arranged and rearranged, filmed and refilmed, one on top of the other, printed in different sizes, all shot from a single camera position. Colours are altered drastically in the reshooting, printing and reprinting stages; shadows appear to further affect colours. The originals are rectangles but once again arranging and rearranging photographs on photographs creates an optical bend, so that the images, many times reproduced, are perceived as trapezoids. They are perceived as—or may now actually be—trapezoids on the larger trapezoidal frame, but when one walks around one can see changes for, at certain angles, they may be perceived as rectangles.

It is easy to become involved in the making of Snow's works,

58

27. *Painting (Closing the Drum Book)*
Photo: T.E. Moore, The Isaacs Gallery

since they are so constructed as to call attention to his procedures. But the making must not be allowed to overshadow the equally important process of perception. For instance, here in *Painting* there is the framing, the rectangle as trapezoid and vice versa, the looking and seeing itself. And when one looks at this work one sees a strange table-like object whose face carries images which resemble a de Stijl or a constructivist canvas gone expressionistic; yet as one takes it in carefully the strange relationship between an order and plan and expression under control of that order assumes a definite shape. This is a photograph far from the composites of Robinson or Rejlander, in which nuances of colour, shading and shape become evident as photographed. *Painting* exists in homage to painting and the perceptual and intellectual traditions to which Snow feels close. It also celebrates the uses to which they can be put in the art of photography, outside of the tradition of the decisive moment.

59

Chapter 4

Metamorphosis of a Spatial Idea:
Wavelength

The freedom of the individual writer lies in his capacity to be timely, to hear the voice of history. In general, creation is an act of historical self-awareness, of locating oneself in the stream of history.

Boris Eichenbaum[1]

In 1955 at the request of Joseph Cornell, Stan Brakhage made *The Wonder Ring,* a film whose ostensible subject was the soon-to-be-destroyed Third Avenue Elevated in New York City. This film initiated Brakhage's shift away from ponderous psychodrama to a concern with seeing. Although he continued to use psychodrama for a time in one form or another, as in the masturbation film *Flesh of Morning* (1956) and in *Wedlock House: An Intercourse* (1959), his involvement with vision began to predominate in his films and his writings at this time. He often combined this with his interest in mythopoetic and psychological structures.[2]

When his *Anticipation of the Night* (1958) was first shown, audiences complained of not being able to see the images because they passed by too quickly or were unclear. In *Cat's Cradle* of the following year, terse and elliptical drama is created through short and punctuated cuts which, in a claustrophobic setting, visually relate and visually confuse the human faces with a cat in heat and patterned wallpaper. One is forced to read the illusions as one would the images of a poem, cross-referencing and going back and rereading. Even more difficult films followed these, testing and challenging the audience's capacity to see.

By 1963 Brakhage had articulated his position in his writings as well as in his films. In *Metaphors on Vision*[3] he spoke of "closed-eye vision"—a somewhat nebulous term which includes hypnogogic vision, day and night dreams, hallucinations, sights which occur under stress or tension, memory and other kinds of imaginings. It is in these ways, according to Brakhage, that one breaks out of the conventionalized modes of seeing through one-point Renaissance perspective and regains the innocent, untrained and expansive capacity of a child's vision. Brakhage the romantic sought to make manifest film metaphors of his own vision through all available means—whether spitting on the lens, using anamorphic lenses and makeshift prisms, scratching and hand painting film, intentionally filming out of focus, employing out-of-date and irregular stock, and consistently shooting with a handheld camera.[4]

Through his film techniques Brakhage consciously allied himself with abstract expressionism, speaking of "gesturing" with his camera and of the camera as an "extension" of his body used to "in-gather" light.[5] The analogy is apt since Brakhage shares with Pollock, Kline and other gesturalists impulsive and deeply emotive roots in work which is romantic, often highly personalized and underpinned with obscure and metaphysical intentions. These artists were also deeply immersed in the materials of their medium and worked to break out of European-inherited traditions into new areas. Brakhage too is very much concerned with the materials of his art but remains primarily a romantic for whom all things seem possible on film.

Like his predecessor Maya Deren and some of his peers such as Kenneth Anger and Gregory Markopoulos, Brakhage fought to have his work recognized. But as he was slowly beginning to be acknowledged, a historical jolt occurred. In 1962 Jonas Mekas initiated the Film-Makers' Cinematheque, virtually the only place where the inchoate American avant-garde film of the 1960s could be seen. It existed in various locations in New York City until 1970, and every American filmmaker whose work was within the purview of the avant-garde had screenings there. It was not long before Andy Warhol began frequenting the Cinematheque, taking in Brakhage, Jack Smith, Kenneth Anger and a range of other artists, and soon launched his own film career. *Kiss, Sleep, Eat* and *Blow-Job,* made in 1963, and *Empire, Henry Geldzahler* and *Couch,* completed in 1964, are all silent films but hardly within the silent aesthetic of Brakhage. They were made with long takes, often with no movement, the camera firmly fixed to its tripod—a bold affront to the image-making in *Dog Star Man, Anticipation of the Night, Window Water Baby Moving, Thigh Line Lyre Triangular* and *Mothlight,* just as Warhol's silkscreen works hang in quiet defiance next to a Pollock, a Rothko, a Kline or a Still. Warhol's image is there, but it is an image recorded continuously over time or loop printed or made by splicing individual takes together one reel after another with end-roll flares. These films were all shot at twenty-four frames per second but projected at eighteen.[6] The loop-printed rolls extended to six hours in *Sleep,* which documents a man's sleep, and eight hours in *Empire,* which records the top of New York's familiar Art Deco Empire State Building.

Brakhage's evangelical mission expressed in his personalized mythology of exquisite images, the rhythms of his elliptical

61

28. Andy Warhol, *Eat*
Photo: Anthology Film Archives

cutting, his sensuous, romantic use of colour and his breaking away from conventional ways of seeing things was undermined by long takes in which the viewer scanned the screen for any change whatsoever. All of Warhol's early silent films which left the Factory were screened at the Cinematheque, and Mekas immediately recognized their importance in his *Village Voice* column. In 1964 *Film Culture* gave the Sixth Independent Film Award to Warhol for *Sleep, Haircut, Eat, Kiss* and *Empire.* The Fourth Award had gone to Brakhage for *The Dead* and *Prelude* and the Fifth to Jack Smith for *Flaming Creatures.* The award citation written by Mekas simply and elegantly summarizes the importance of Warhol's early silent films. It reads in part:

Andy Warhol is taking cinema back to its origins, to the days of Lumière, for a rejuvenation and a cleansing. In his work, he has abandoned all the "cinematic" form and subject adornment that cinema had gathered around itself until now. He has focused his lens on the plainest images possible . . . . A strange thing occurs. The world becomes transposed, intensified, electrified. We see it sharper than before.

And then Mekas predicts some of what was to come and is now a part of history:

As a result of Andy Warhol's work, we are going to see soon these simple phenomena, like Eating, or Trees, or Sunrise filmed by a number of different artists, each time differently, each time a new Tree, a new Eating, a new Sunrise. Some of them will be bad, some good, some mediocre, like any other movie—and somebody will make a masterpiece. In any case, it will be a new adventure; the world seen through a consciousness that is not running after big dramatic events but is focused on more subtle changes and nuances. Andy Warhol's cinema is a meditation on the objective world.[7]

In 1965-66 George Landow, an artist whose contributions are just now beginning to be acknowledged, made his four-and-a-half minute loop-printed *Film in Which There Appear Sprocket Holes, Edge Lettering, Dirt Particles, etc.,* followed in 1966-67 by a twenty-minute version using the same footage. Tony Conrad and Paul Sharits made their first flicker films in 1966. And at Knokke-Le-Zoute, Belgium, in the Christmas-New Year week of 1967-68, Michael Snow's *Wavelength* (1966-67) took the Grand Prize in the Fourth International Experimental Film Festival. The film fulfilled something of the prophecy offered by Mekas in his Sixth Independent Award citation to Warhol.

In Brakhage, Warhol, Snow and the other artists just mentioned, one senses the historical awareness and the self-awareness referred to in the Eichenbaum passage at the beginning of this chapter. This twin consciousness is a prerequisite for serious

29. Stan Brakhage, *Mothlight*
Photo: Anthology Film Archives

practice of the arts in this century. Just as Brakhage was cognizant of what preceded and surrounded him in film and the related art environment, Warhol in turn absorbed Brakhage, Jack Smith, Ron Rice, Kenneth Anger and others. The flicker works, Landow's films and *Wavelength* were made in a world conscious of both Brakhage and Warhol. The focus of these works shifted beyond Warhol and became more literalist and minimalist, more exploratory and self-questioning, as was occurring in painting and sculpture at that time.

Wavelength marks the beginning of Snow's significant film contribution, an essential part of which is his exploration of the possibilities of camera movement. It also marks a major change in Snow's art. In it were synthesized elements of his work not previously brought together. He says: "Well, *Wavelength* was done in 1966. It was one of those personal crisis things, I tried to put a lot in it. I tried to solve a lot of things for myself in it . . . tried

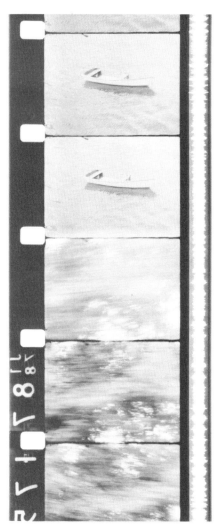

30. *New York Eye and Ear Control*
Photo: Michael Snow

to bring some things together that seemed to be separate in my work but that I felt ought to be brought together." But it is necessary to understand how this occurs and why. Snow continues in the same interview: "*Wavelength* was a culmination of the serial and variation method that happened in the 'Walking Woman' works over a period of five or six years, along with ideas about time that basically came from music and other things that were personal. It was really very important to me in my own life."[8] But before *Wavelength* is examined it is useful to look at Snow's earlier film of 1964, *New York Eye and Ear Control* (referred to in its credits as "A Walking Woman Work") because of the presence of nascent film preoccupations developed and refined upon in later works.

New York Eye and Ear Control is organized around a series of binary relationships. Snow speaks of one of these as the romantic and classic represented respectively by the jazz sound track and the Walking Woman cut-out. "There's a terrific separation between the music, which is very, very personal expression, full of cries and yells and so on, and is very spontaneous, and images which are calm, single spaced and placed [*sic*] things of long duration."[9]

For the ear: the jazz track is contrasted with two clear and pronounced silences. For the eye: country and seascape are contrasted with cityscape, outdoor with indoor spaces, light with dark images and exposures, background and deep spaces with foreground and flat or two-dimensional spaces, moving camera or movement in the frame with stationary camera or stilled images, and figure with ground. A series of portraits of women is followed by portraits of men, and in each group there are both black and white people.

In *New York Eye and Ear Control* the Walking Woman is seen perhaps 70-75 per cent of the time. After a nine-line free verse prologue and credits,[10] a solid-white Walking Woman cut-out appears on a black background. This long take terminates in end-roll flares and dots after which the camera moves to an overexposed sky in search of the missing cut-out. In this section the Walking Woman usually appears in either black or white against backgrounds of sky, water, beach or trees, in long or medium-long shots. A tracking shot functions as a transition from country and seascape to a segment of cityscape. In the city the camera follows a passenger being picked up at a curb and then, in a matching shot, left off at another curb in lower Manhattan. With the tracking camera the jazz heard earlier resumes and continues to the end of the film. Because of the overall asymmetry of *New York Eye and Ear Control,* its symmetrical centre may go unnoticed. It continues the juxtapositions of non-urban versus urban environments, beginning with a black Walking Woman in foreground backed by a segment of New York skyscrapers. In this approximately two-minute-long shot the background becomes progressively lighter until the image bleaches out to dawn. The Walking Woman in foreground is set against the following long shot of the Walking Woman in seascape, which initially appears upside down in the exact middle of the film, barely long enough to be identified, then right side up. This take lasts two minutes and like its complement also fades to white. The Walking Woman is then washed over with sand, burned, swung in pendulum fasion, run over by a car and hung. The film moves indoors for the two portrait sections—the first with Walking Woman cut-outs and live women shot in profile, the second with full-face portraits of black and white men in medium-close to close-up shots against different backgrounds, in granular images and dark exposures. A black man and a white woman make love and the film ends with a nervous camera movement over rows of Walking Woman figures.[11]

New York Eye and Ear Control contains a realism of practice already seen in some of Snow's earlier works, such as *Lac Clair*. For example, one finds under- and overexposed shots altering the space of the image, end-roll flares, dots and splice marks, prominently granular images and passages of single takes up to two minutes long—a practice unusual for the time (1964) except in the films of Warhol. Flatness, so significant in Snow's later film and photographic work, is also accentuated here. The choices of spaces—beach with rock, sky, water, clustered foilage, cluttered line of skyscrapers and walls—together with the camera angles and the "imperfect" light exposures, all work formally away from the illusion of depth toward flatness. The Walking Woman cut-out appears flush to the surface of the screen or in long shot against a background, its abbreviated extremities emphasizing framing in both cases.

New York Eye and Ear Control does not have the clarity and legibility of Snow's later work, however. It is neither linear nor casual nor minimal nor narrative. One might refer to it as poetic, with the nine-line free verse at the beginning offering a clue to the form which follows: the Walking Woman serving visually as the flat refrain, serially recurring and converted almost to stanzas when it makes its persistent appearances in the several long takes. Yet the label *poetic* may be a rationalization of the basic problem of the film's structure. The overall visual structure, instead of balancing with the jazz track, becomes romantic, dominating the controlling classical images of the Walking Woman. The film is expressive and evocative, but of what?

John Cage's comments on a situation similar to Snow's are

illuminating. Speaking of the dilemma he encountered in composing *The Perilous Night* (1945) he stated: "I had poured a great deal of emotion into the piece and obviously I wasn't communicating this at all. Or else, I thought, if I were communicating then all artists must be speaking a different language, and thus speaking only for themselves. The whole musical situation struck me more and more as a Tower of Babel."[12] Cage gradually rejected expression in this arbitrary sense as a motivation for his music.

It is not only the overall structure of *New York Eye and Ear Control* but also the Walking Woman which is at issue. While it is the film's central support it is also ultimately its undoing. The figure of the Walking Woman is caught between two roles, one as sculpture and the other as vehicle for filmic ideas. Ultimately it seems more illustrative of the former.

In the six-year Walking Woman project Snow made use of series, serial, replication, variation and permutation. In *New York Eye and Ear Control* the persistent figure unites opposite and disparate kinds of spaces—flat and deep, rural and urban. From Snow's use of the Walking Woman here one can extrapolate to his use of the camera and time in *Wavelength,* through which the Walking Woman figure is metamorphosed into a spatio-temporal formal dimension.

In a letter to Jonas Mekas and P. Adams Sitney, Snow writes:

Now: one of the subjects of or one of the things *Wavelength* attempts to be is a "balancing" of different orders, classes of events and protagonists. The image of the yellow chair has as much "value" in its own world as the girl closing the window. The film events are not hierarchial but are chosen from a kind of scale of mobility that runs from pure light events, the various perceptions of the room, to the images of moving human beings.[13]

In this passage two notions are especially significant: balance and non-hierarchical event. Regarding the latter one is reminded of Robbe-Grillet in whose novels and essays about writing, objects and persons are given equivalent significance, one class no more important than another. This and the idea of balancing, an already important concept in *New York Eye and Ear Control,* work together in *Wavelength.* Snow uses the term *balance* or a synonym for it at least eight times when speaking of *Wavelength* in the issue of *Film Culture* that includes the letter just quoted from, an interview and his famous Knokke statement. In the last Snow writes:

Wavelength was shot in one week Dec. '66 preceded by a year of notes, thots [*sic*], mutterings. It was edited and first print seen in May '67. I

66

wanted to make a summation of my nervous system, religious inklings, and aesthetic ideas. I was thinking of planning for a time monument in which the beauty and sadness of equivalence would be celebrated, thinking of trying to make a definitive statement of pure Film space and time, a balancing of "illusion" and "fact", all about seeing. The space starts at the camera (spectator's) eye, is in the air, then is on the screen, then is within the screen (the mind).

The film is a continuous zoom which takes 45 minutes to go from its widest field to its smallest and final field. It was shot with a fixed camera from one end of an 80 foot loft, shooting the other end, a row of windows and the street. This, the setting, and the action which takes place there are cosmically equivalent. The room (and the zoom) are interrupted by 4 human events including a death. The sound on these occasions is sync sound, music and speech occurring simultaneously with an electronic sound, a sine wave, which goes from its lowest (50 cycles per second) note to its highest (12000 c.p.s.) in 40 minutes. It is a total glissando while the film is a crescendo and a dispersed spectrum which attempts to utilize the gifts of both prophecy and memory which only film and music have to offer.[14]

What is meant by "cosmically equivalent"? Can one measure the "beauty and sadness of equivalence" or a "time monument" housing them? Who but the artist himself is able to gauge the success or failure of such transcendent, ineffable intentions? Yet while he can write of these things Snow can also precisely describe the length of the loft, the number of human incidents and sound elements, and the c.p.s. of the sine wave from start to finish. His words reflect the double direction of the film—the evocative, expressive, and apparently arbitrary balanced with the exploratory and analytical, something he had striven for but not attained in *New York Eye and Ear Control.*

In his letter to Sitney and Mekas, Snow speaks of improvising in the course of shooting *Wavelength* simply because he felt like it. Yet this improvisation occurred only after the year's planning and preparation. In the *Film Culture* interview he repeats in slightly, but significantly, different form a notion from his Knokke statement. "I meant it as a summation of everything that I've thought about, everything." And he continues, responding first to Sitney's question about the zoom: "It [the zoom and the film] is attempting to balance out in a way all the so-called realities there involved in the issue of making a film. I thought that maybe the issues hadn't really been stated clearly about film in the same sort of way—now this is presumptuous, but to say— in the way Cézanne, say, made a balance between the coloured goo that he used, which is what you see if you look at it in that way, and the forms that you see in their illusory space."[15]

Stan Brakhage had already explored space, time, light and film materials, but as Snow wondered, naming no names, perhaps the "issues" had not been dealt with clearly enough. "Issue" suggests examination, exploration, analysis of given questions and the pursuit of new ones. Snow's investigation becomes both epistemological and ontological as he deals with the dialectics of various film questions. Brakhage, like the abstract expressionists with whom he allies himself, is concerned with the materials of his art, but his films are often dominated by a romantic subjectivity. They become repositories for his inspired and mythopoetic vision in abstruse and recondite images. In contrast, samples of Snow's own non-film work following *Lac Clair* indicate, as has been pointed out, his attempt to balance expressiveness with research and exploration. In *Wavelength* he finally sums up and clarifies these issues. The nature and look of the image in *Wavelength,* the attitude toward it and consequently the perceiver's relationship to it become qualitatively different from what one had become accustomed to in Brakhage.

In abstract expressionism brush strokes often become the measure of autobiography in the same way that Brakhage's use of his camera conveys emotional and personal states. Apropos Pollock and de Kooning, Lawrence Alloway states that "Abstract Expressionism shares with 'action' [painting] a similar over-emphasis on work-procedures, defining the work of art as a seismic record of the artist's anxiety."[16] Yet while a colour field painter like Barnett Newman is often subsumed under the abstract expressionist label, he has neither a vigorous emphasis on work procedures nor brush strokes as autobiographical gesture. Nevertheless, Newman stands somewhere in the middle, as Alloway describes him in the same essay, with "art predicated on expression and art as an object."[17] His *Stations of the Cross* are non-inconographic yet the title is referential and evocative. Newman, although he worked exclusively in colour field abstraction, suggests a useful kind of analogy to Snow; like the elder Newman, Snow's work shares a double stress. In contrast, a similar analogy might link Pollock and Brakhage.

The connection to Newman is only by analogy, however. Snow is dealing with the representational as a given. The issues generated by film time and space are a mixture of fact and illusion, reality and artifice. Art as "expression and art as an object" suggests just one of the sets of dialectics at work here, and expression-evocation versus exploration-analysis another.

These oppositions become more apparent when an elaboration is made of Snow's Knokke description. Dating at least from the *Right Reader* performance and the film *Short Shave* (both 1965), Snow has used sheets of coloured transparencies. They occupy a significant place in *Wavelength* as they do in other of his

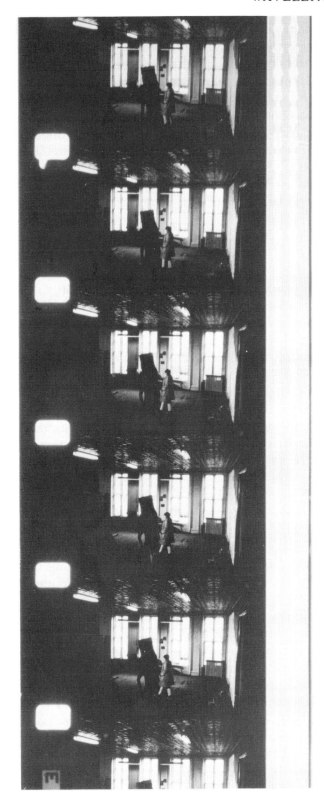

film and non-film works which will be looked at in a subsequent chapter. Snow introduces *Wavelength* with a very brief section first of translucent orange interrupted by flash credits, a barely legible title and then more colour, after which the room appears accompanied by ambient sound.

The metamorphosis of the image begins and the zoom frames the length of the loft, the four large windows at its opposite end and beyond. Each window consists of eight panes. At what becomes the centre of the wall between two windows is a bright yellow vinyl-covered kitchen chair. Its slightly curved contour contrasts with the angularity of window frames, fluorescent light fixtures, desk and radiator, and its colour stands in high relief against the white walls, black desk, and the soon-to-be-carried-in cool blue bookcase. The camera is positioned high on a platform and set at an angle framing an area just slightly to the right of centre. The shooting angle and the general rectilinearity of the objects, with the curved yellow chair placed at a slight bias to the wall, establish a tension within the room and along the zoom. The wide angle of the zoom picks up the line of the wall on the right, exaggerating the space and length of the loft. Yet in contrast to this depth the windowed wall and the facades and signs across the street framed by the windows stress flatness, anticipating what is to come. It gradually becomes clear that the zoom is aiming toward the middle of the wall where the chair is located. Above the chair and fastened to the wall are three of what can only be awkwardly described at this point in the zoom as rectangles.

An absolutely accurate description of *Wavelength* measured in feet or minutes will not be equivalent to a phenomenological one for it is impossible to say precisely when one realizes certain of the changes in the film. Suddenly it is dark outside or then light again. When is the right wall eliminated? Or the bookcase on the left? One of the pictures on the wall is legible; now it is not; another is now; and so on. As in minimal art, with which *Wavelength* shares some affinities, much is posited on the transaction between viewer and the work of art.

Shortly after the image of the loft appears, footsteps are heard. It is daytime. A woman enters the frame from bottom left followed by two men carrying in the light blue bookcase. They place it where she directs and all three leave quickly. The zoom continues slowly. The woman reenters with a companion, both carrying coffee cups. The former goes to the radio and turns on "Strawberry Fields Forever," while the other pushes a window nearly closed and sits on the sill. On the title phrase "Strawberry Fields Forever" there is a quick but intense red transparency over

33. *Wavelength*
photo: The National Gallery of Canada

the image of the loft. Immediately after this the second woman rises and walks out while the first stands at the radio for a time, turns it off and also leaves. Both exit at the bottom of the frame.

Ambient sounds stop when the sine wave begins. At the quick flicker section of solid red and black colour frames one notices "discrepancies" in the room's realistic space, though the short colour flashes and changes of exposure during the bookcase event have already questioned assumptions about what the film is and what it documents. The alterations of the image are the events which Snow wishes one to consider in equivalence with the "human events" but which also enhance the difficulty of description. The entrance of the sine with the flicker segment becomes dramatic in its abruptness and force. Colour negative follows for about one hundred feet. Then the image of the loft briefly disappears, replaced by clear leader, creating a screen of white light, to reappear filtered in a dark, cold green. There are fades, underexposed and overexposed footage, more flicker. Such vicissitudes are constantly measuring and assessing the space of the loft and flattening and asserting the existence of the image as film in its own present tense.

71

There is a cold blue-filtered length of film emphasizing the granularity of the film stock which, one only realizes later, ends the continuous daytime section, for now it is dark outside. A crash, siren, shots and stumbling are heard accompanied by a short red flicker pattern as a man enters the frame and falls. A siren is heard again along with the continuing sine as the zoom passes over the body and flickering continues briefly during and after the man's fall.

More filtered, over- and underexposed and granular passages follow, along with fades, changes in film stock and alterations in the light within and outside of the loft. A quick superimposition takes the perceiver to an earlier part of the film and room. No sooner does one realize that it is light outdoors than it becomes dark again as the last human event takes place. A woman enters bottom right side of the frame, turns and pauses over what would be the body now long out of camera range, goes to the telephone at the desk, dials and addresses "Richard." She tells him that there is a man on the floor who is not drunk but dead, asks that he meet her downstairs and then hurriedly leaves the ever shrinking space. Elliptically, in black and white superimposed flashes, her movements are immediately recapitulated silently over the zoom's and the sine's progression.

All the while the zoom narrows in more and more toward the wall with the chair in front of it. The rectangles become identifiable as pictures tacked up on the wall. They are crucial to the film, as is the way they are slowly perceived. It is at least one-third of the way into the film before one can identify two Walking Woman cut-outs and still later, above and adjacent to them, two photographs of a woman walking down a street. Changes in light and exposure setting and various colour transparencies intermittently obscure the already difficult-to-perceive photographs. The zoom is ultimately edging toward the final picture placed below the others, the reading of which is still ambiguous; it appears dark and flat and illegible until well into the last half of the film when one begins to see it variously as a sandy beach, sunset, perhaps waves, depending upon the shooting conditions. Finally one begins to read it for what it is: a still of waves with neither shore nor horizon.

As the zoom presses forward the kitchen chair is finally eliminated, although it returns briefly later when Snow cuts back to an earlier time and space on the zoom. Gradually the two photographs of the woman on the street and then the Walking Woman cut-outs are omitted. Now the windows vanish. The succession of superimpositions ends. For a brief flash a halo effect surrounds the remaining photograph, and then Snow dissolves to a full frame of the waves. The persistent sound of the sine wave, whose pitch continues cycling higher and higher, splits itself up at this range and then stops before the image does. The waves are brought out of focus and *Wavelength* ends.[18].

Wavelength hinges on the zoom as does all discussion of it. Only as the zoom very slowly edges forward does the perceiver become aware of the Walking Woman figures on the wall. Later the figures are removed from view by the zoom's movement. Yet the idea of the Walking Woman has not been eliminated but instead transformed. Now on film and in film terms the zoom becomes formally and methodologically what Snow attempted through the cut-out figure of the Walking Woman in various purely spatial media and which, when used in his earlier film, *New York Eye and Ear Control,* was less than successful. Drawn from imagination the Walking Woman became the given for replication, series, serial and variation.[19] Here the zoom becomes the given. It extends the graphic and purely spatial aspect into time; objects as multiples in space through time are translated by analogy into a continuity along a line in time and through space on the zoom. This is complemented by sound in the sine wave, the ear's equivalent to the zoom.

From replication and the serial analogy appropriate to the zoom one returns to the nonhierarchical. Like Robbe-Grillet Snow spoke of not wanting to create a hierarchy of relationships. The idea of the nonhierarchical also appears in minimal art, a phenomenon connected in attitude and sensibility to the new novel and Robbe-Grillet. Using the term *wholistic* [holistic] rather than nonhierarchical, Lawrence Alloway describes it: "The formal difference between wholistic and hierarchic form is often described as 'relational' and 'nonrelational.' Relational refers to paintings like that of the earlier geometric artists, which are subdivided and balanced with a hierarchy of forms, large, medium, small. Nonrelational, on the contrary, refers to unmodulated monochromes, completely symmetrical layouts, or unaccented grids. In fact, of course, relationships are those of continuity and repetition rather than of contrast and interplay."[20]

As Snow so succinctly states: "Events take time. Events take place."[21] It is by way of the zoom that events in *Wavelength* are made nonhierarchical. The zoom becomes the spatio-temporal analogue for the unitary or nonrelational and purely spatial form in painting and sculpture. Its continuity makes out of the space of the room an event in time which in its turn, then, is also nonhierarchical. The zoom's very unity operates against a

73

34, 35. *Wavelength*
Photo: The National Gallery of Canada

hierarchy of events and orders of events along its movement in time. It stops for nothing—neither "death" nor colour change nor sound.

Yet Snow has it both ways. *Wavelength* still contains "windows to the world," ambient sound and evocative uses of colour. In this way it deviates from the major tenets of minimal art which might allow allusions to other paintings or sculptures as part of a series but which shun illusion and focus on the object as finished product without traces of facture. In *Wavelength* Snow deals with representational illusions and the system of accompanying beliefs with which one approaches a "film." He treats process through the nature of the zoom, at the same time that he offers means of perceiving the film as object in its own time, in and for itself.

While the zoom embodies the transformation from an earlier aesthetic preoccupation of Snow's and bears relationships to minimal art, it has its own history as film technology and potential aesthetic device. The zoom lens has been used professionally only since the late 1940s, although it had been know for at least twenty years prior to that in a non-marketable form. In *American Cinematographer Manual* an expert writes: "Leaving out the aesthetic value of the zoom lens and the pros and cons regarding its single view point, gradual compression of foreground subject and background, and other pictorial disadvantages—there is no doubt that the zoom lens is here to stay!

"The ability of the zoom lens to continuously vary the area photographically simplifies certain aspects of filming. The cinematographer can instantly choose the field of view he wishes, set his focus and aperture, and then concentrate on framing and composing the scene as it progresses."[22]

With the zoom Snow is exploring a facet of film and its technology, but does more than that. By exaggerating and protracting the zoom, Snow challenges and reverses its so-called aesthetic disadvantages as he explores another attitude toward it.

Moreover, just as the Walking Woman project rested on an a priori decision to use a particular form, *Wavelength* uses a technical device which becomes an aesthetic constant. As will be discussed in connection with ←——→ and *La Région Centrale,* Snow places more and more importance on choices about machinery and technology. In those two works and in part in *Wavelength* the burden of the "art-act" shifts progressively away from expression to an exploration by means of the medium itself and a stress on the artist's ideas and decisions rather than craft and workmanship. Snow's use of the zoom and subsequent technical means are elements of his work which emphasize more

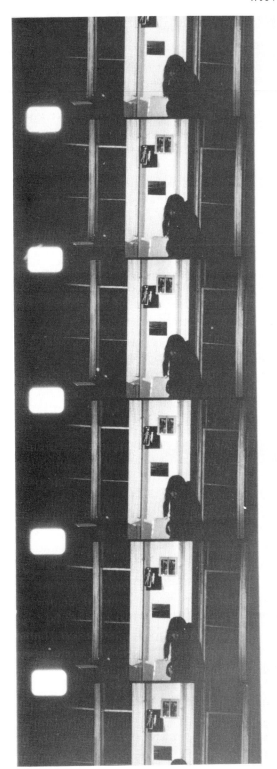

and more his distance from Brakhage. Significantly, Brakhage entitles the second part of *Metaphors on Vision* "My Eye," and elsewhere speaks of the camera as an extension of himself. Snow, in his Knokke description of *Wavelength,* equates the camera's eye with the spectator's, opening up another kind of relationship between film and perceiver. While the recondite, private vision and emphatic autobiographical gesture is eliminated in Snow, his work is still expressive and no less personal than Brakhage's. Snow takes his place within a tradition of art endeavor inspired by Duchamp, continued through Cage into minimal, process and conceptual art where the signature of the personal shifts to ideas, choices and decisions.

The expert quoted above could never have imagined in his prediction how Snow would "concentrate on framing" as the zoom progressed. Through the very nature of its intensity and slow movement the zoom hyperbolizes aspects of the frame and framing. One becomes involved with on-screen space and that passage of space slipping off screen, as one thinks of the dimensions of the film frame and beyond.[23] The zoom's framing is further emphasized, reiterated and complemented by the battery of window frames and the three sets of pictures on the wall which frame themselves. As one tries to read the framed pictures on the wall one becomes aware of the tension of the compressing zoom closing in on and flattening the space more and more, an effect increased by the already described rectilinearity of the room with its odd protagonist, the curved yellow chair. The steadily rising sine wave adds to this tension in the frame while the ambient noises point outside of that space.

Space and framing are examined through the zoom but also through the use of narrative. *Wavelength* questions narrative conventions and traditions. In the four human events which occur along the zoom's progression, the first and second can be connected by the appearance of the same woman in both, and the third and fourth by the telephone call. One can construct a story in which there is neither beginning, middle nor end, only events along the zoom from its start to finish, from one field of space slowly shifting to another. But along Snow's "scale of mobility" tension builds up and the sounds and entrance and fall of the man followed later by the woman's movements become, in context, dramatic. All the while the viewers must participate, filling-in and creating the narrative themselves.

Conventions of sound and colour are, in Shklovsky's terms, "laid bare" or "revealed." On- and off-screen ambient sound extends the space of the film and enhances the narrative. Sync sound is present yet at times Snow makes peculiar, selective use of it. When the woman lowers the window all sounds stop except for the radio, and as she leaves her footsteps are not heard; yet when her companion turns off the radio and departs her steps and the sounds from outside are once again audible. Later sound is heard only as the woman reaches and pivots around to look at the off-screen body. The wild track preceding the man's entrance sounds tinny and his fall seems slightly out of sync. In several instances Snow uses colours for their conventional value in a kind of symbolist cliché. On "Strawberry Fields Forever" there are red flashes, and again on the gun shots and crashing prior to, during and after the man's fall. Devoid of human activity the loft appears in cold green and later cold blue tint. Still later are the black and white recapitulation shots of the woman at the telephone which suggest both memory and a certain ghostliness.

Wavelength incorporates both the linear and the narrative. Linearity is traditionally used to describe plot based on causality, moving from beginning to middle to end. In *Wavelength* one might speak of causality in relationship to the phone conversation, but one fails to make a story in the conventional sense of the human events which occur. Narrative linearity is for all practical purposes mocked. In its place *Wavelength* uses a literal line in time and space on the zoom along which events occur, the vector of the zoom stopping for nothing, even a falling body, as it simply passes over it, eliminating it from frame.

Snow's words "Events take time. Events take place" describe literally what happens in *Wavelength*. The film narrates the time and space of the loft which becomes an event through the moving zoom, and the human events become merely a part of the larger story. Snow's film can be seen as a study of space and time in which the two become equivalent, actualizing the famous but little explored or discussed idea of Erwin Panofsky about the "spatialization of time" and the "dynamization of space."[24] The movement of the zoom is the length and extent of the film and the time of the film measures the space of the room. Yet Snow is not dealing with "real time," nor is there any attempt to suggest this as the time passes from day to night to day to night, the zoom all the while persisting forward.

Wavelength's relationship to Robbe-Grillet now becomes clearer. In his novels the study and examination of objects constitutes the narrative as he disposes of anthropocentricity and traditional neohumanism with its literary trappings of character development and other conventions.

If, as Snow suggests, *Wavelength* is more like Vermeer than Cézanne, he still has it both ways. Perhaps it is like Vermeer in its concentration on detail in a highly illusionistic space, but at the same time it is like Cézanne for its planar qualities and calculated flatness pulling away from the three-dimensional, even while acknowledging it. For in closing in on the space, in de-hierarchizing the events along the zoom, in concentrating attention through zoom and sine wave fixed in the slowly changing frame, Snow sets up in the oscillation between the representational and the abstract a dialogue between reality and film. He works to fulfill his aspiration of making "a definitive statement of pure film space and time, a balancing of 'illusion' and 'fact,' all about seeing."

Strong transparent colours and pronounced granularity flatten the image. Perspective is distorted by flickering colours and flickering exposure patterns. Other events also distort perspective: colour negative, black and white footage, clear footage, pseudo wipes—transparencies seen being put in front of or removed from over the lens/screen, fades, superimpositions, flares, end roll dots and varying lighting conditions along with changes in exposure. As one concentrates on the intensity and direction of the zoom, the image of the room is erupted, tipped, caught between the fact of the flat screen and the illusion of depth until finally there is no room to be represented, as "space as milieu" is metamorphosized into "space as limit" on the white screen.[25]

Unlike Bazin, Snow does not permit or even wish for an asymptotic relationship between film and the world. Despite the representational nature of the room image, the zoom works subtly to stylize, formalize and abstract the image against the very grain of reality. While there is no "montage" there is "cutting" along the zoom and no attempt is made to camouflage discontinuities. As Snow describes it he had to start shooting the film in about the middle of the zoom just prior to the entrance and fall of the man played by Hollis Frampton, since Frampton was only available on that particular day. Snow then had to continue from that point on the zoom. Moreover, the borrowed camera and zoom lens had to be disassembled after each shooting. The breaks are clear: a momentary shift to what looks like a frontal shot, the dissolve to full frame of the wave, as well as the appearance of colour negative, clear leader, transparencies and other devices already described. These all function to distance the viewer and point reflexively to the film as object. Actually and metaphorically the zoom suggests analysis and exploration of Snow's "aesthetic ideas" in opposition to those more evocative, visionary ideas he refers to as a "summation" of his "nervous system, religious inklings," and a celebration of the "beauty and sadness of equivalence" in a "time monument." *Wavelength* reverses commercial film conventions while playing against the avant-garde represented by the romanticism of Brakhage in breaking down expectations and forcing one to perceive, to think and rethink.

If minimal art essentially shunned metaphor, *Wavelength* does not. Even as film-object existing literally in present time and space, *Wavelength* employs metaphors about reading and seeing. Snow's photograph of waves is carefully and consciously placed on the wall as are the other pictures. The images become legible gradually and one at a time—first the Walking Woman cut-outs, then the photographs of a woman on the street, then the photograph of waves. The pairs of walking images are a metaphor for a reading of the film, suggesting in their contrast between flat, cut-out, partial abstraction and full photographic representation the dialectics of the film, and indeed of all film. When the wave image is finally read, first the street figures and then the Walking Woman cut-outs have been eliminated. The title embraces not merely sine wave, colour, and in a metaphoric sense the space in time of the zoom, but also literally the photograph of waves. The waves themselves carry a double suggestion: they are expansive and endless, but also frozen and bear no trace of horizon nor other visual clue to depth. Finally the photograph is taken out of focus and into whiteness and complete flatness.

In *Wavelength* the Walking Woman is metamorphosized into the formal device of the zoom, but is also still present on the wall as Snow's signature and as a dialectic with the photographs of a woman on the street. The other images are also a clue pointing both literally and metaphorically to the difficulty of perception and to the active process involved in consciousness as one constantly strives to read, adjust, readjust, to constitute and to reflect on the objects once they are brought into the range of consciousness.

Proceeding through the space and time of *Wavelength,* one is involved in the art "object" and the art "expression." As one strains to see the images on the wall at the other end of the loft, one reads variables and events along the zoom for forty-five minutes. One only knows the film through that line in time which ends in whiteness and flatness after passing through and analyzing a room and various reactions to it. One only knows *Wavelength* through the nuances along the way and the triad of images at the end. Once they are all read they refer back to the phenomenological act of constituting *Wavelength* in perception, in experience.[26]

Chapter 5

Autobiography and the Literal Imagination

Stan Brakhage was the most important figure in the American avant-garde film from 1958 when his *Anticipation of the Night* first appeared through the mid-1960s. But in the late sixties Snow took over this role, the film work of Warhol having exerted a strong influence in the earlier part of the decade. I continue to refer to Brakhage in this discussion of Snow because their respective concerns, attitudes and sensibilities not only differ one from another but are in all essentials at odds. In the opposition Brakhage's traditional role as romantic artist only accentuates Snow's significantly different place in the film avant-garde, and one which is much more difficult to grasp.

In introducing Snow earlier I spoke briefly of his idiosyncratic and nonromantic uses of autobiography in his art, an art which in turn reveals nothing about the man himself. Here I will look further at autobiography and the everyday as subject matter in Snow's art, his exploratory and analytical camera techniques, and his devices of description and literalization. These elements which may appear unrelated do in fact function together in the construction of a distanced and usually formal art.

Again a useful comparison can be drawn between Brakhage and Snow. In the previous chapter I mentioned Brakhage's expressive notion of the camera as an extension of his body in contrast to Snow's analytical camera. Now I want to examine how the respective uses of autobiography and the everyday in each are closely related to their particular camera techniques.

Brakhage's employment of autobiography and the everyday has its analogues in literature, particularly romantic literature. He draws materials from his own as well as his family's life. The term *home movie* is almost an encomium in his vocabulary, for his work helped to legitimize the quotidian in both 8mm and 16mm filmmaking. The psychological and even the mythological often enter his milieu: for example, the myth of the struggling artist (Brakhage as woodsman in *Dog Star Man,* 1961-64); psychological exploration of masturbation (*Flesh of Morning,* 1956); and the trauma of wedlock and identification with another married couple (*Cat's Cradle,* 1959).[1] His comments on *Wedlock House: An Intercourse,* also of 1959, reveal his strong feeling of power, his belief in a vital tie between film and life, his sense of "black magic" in the editing of the film and his fear of how the work might affect his life and love relationship with his wife, Jane.

Looking at the images and getting only horror, I was afraid of editing, afraid that I would be performing some black magic act, cursing what little chance we had for making a love structure out of our life together. For months I resisted, resisted, I struggled with that footage trying to edit it, you know, trying to get it balanced. Finally I gave up and said, "If horror is what it is, then I will go straight into it." It was like breaking through a sound barrier: suddenly the total beauty of what happened to us right straight off the battleground of our lives was what structured and made true scenes in these flashes.[2]

Here it seems clear that for Brakhage as maker his film functions psychologically as a form of catharsis. Like his gesturing camera, his attitude toward autobiography is connected to the idea that film as art is self-expression.

Snow, however, incorporates autobiography in anomalous ways which often force one to reconsider and to redefine it. His comments on *Side Seat Paintings Slides Sound Film* are illuminating: "It came out of doing my book, *A Survey,* for the Ontario Art Gallery show, in February, 1970. And also the whole retrospective thing that made me look back at my work for the first time. I was interested in using the records of old work as the material for new works. The book uses still photos. The film uses slides."[3] Snow incorporates objects from his life as artist—older art, art-making materials and related elements—into new art.

Other examples will make this clearer. In *A Casing Shelved* (1970) a slide of a bookcase filled with old art-making and related objects is projected while Snow, on audiotape, discusses for forty-six minutes the contents of the shelves; Walking Woman cut-outs are tacked to the wall in *Wavelength; De La* (1969-72), the video installation, makes use of the machinery from *La Région Centrale;* the bright yellow chair of *Wavelength* appears as prominent protagonist in a brief segment of *"Rameau's Nephew" (Thanx to Dennis Young)* by *Wilma Schoen,* while the blue bookcase from *Wavelength* is the casing of *A Casing Shelved,* which the artist points out in his narration for this last piece. Snow often employs gels or transparencies which, in addition to serving as formal device or technique, refer to earlier works and call attention to this general motif weaving through them. In *Sink* (1970) and *Untitled Slidelength* (1969-71), for example, some of the transparencies from *Wavelength* are utilized.

Authorization (1969) and *Venetian Blind* (1970) demonstrate another use of autobiographical material. Each is a series of self-portraits shot with a Polaroid camera, formalized and distanced, containing puns. And *Michael Snow/A Survey* is more than an exhibition catalogue.

In striking contrast to Brakhage, Snow employs autobiography literally, keeping it on the surface where it takes on meanings that are neither psychological nor mythological. It becomes a key to understanding Snow's work and Snow as working artist, whereas the man himself remains outside, even in *Michael Snow/A Survey,* with no intimate or highly personalized information given. Brakhage, on the other hand, proclaims the camera as an extension of himself, his imposing ego dominating his *oeuvre* in nineteenth-century romantic style.

Five of Snow's short single-screen films are good examples of how his use of autobiography and the everyday relate to his camera practices. Three of these were made with a stationary camera—*One Second in Montreal, Side Seat Paintings Slides Sound Film* and *Dripping Water,* and two were shot with camera movement—*Standard Time* and *Breakfast.* Earlier in connection with *One Second in Montreal* it was shown that Snow's use of found objects is not unlike his manipulation of previously made art in the construction of new work. *Dripping Water* of 1969 (made in collaboration with Joyce Wieland) and *Side Seat Paintings Slides Sound Film* of the following year also incorporate other work into new art.

In *Side Seat Paintings Slides Sound Film,* Snow teases the viewer with his framing. The title names/describes the elements in the film. Snow set up his camera at an angle to the screen on which he projected and filmed 35mm slides of his paintings which extend, not entirely chronologically, from 1951 to 1965. The film captures this uncomfortable angle, giving the perceiver the sensation of viewing the images from a side seat. For each slide Snow recites title, date, materials and dimensions, but despite this last information, any real sense of painting size is confounded by slide and film image scale. All clues are further confused and even vitiated as Snow quickly indicates that his paintings must not be viewed as subject of the film; instead they are material from which a new work in another medium has been made. For the film Snow uses a single synchronous visual-sound recording system. He begins at twenty-four frames per second so that the exposure and sound recording are what can be referred to as normal. Gradually the images darken, the voice slows down, until there are long pauses on the soundtrack. Along with Snow's voice with its variations in pitch, one hears the slide machine's motor and slides clicking in and out of place in their carrousel. As the sound speeds up the speech becomes unintelligible, the images gradually lighten and finally are no longer recognizable. Through it all, of course, the slides continue to be projected at their constant angle. The varying lightness and

36. Above left, *A Casing Shelved*
Photo: The National Gallery of Canada

37. Below left, *Side Seat Paintings Slides Sound Film*
Photo: Michael Snow

38. Above, *Venetian Blind*
Photo: Nathan Rabin, Bykert Gallery

darkness of the slides not only flattens the images of the paintings but also creates the illusion that the angles of slide projection change. From the progressively slower and lower voice, slower machine sounds and darker images the system cuts up to light images and higher and faster sounds, back again to slower audio and darkening screen. But just as one has deciphered the collaborative system, it breaks apart. The voice is slow and low but the picture light. On the very last slide Snow's speech is recorded at a normal speed as the image gradually fades into total whiteness. A hand returns the titled and dated film can to the place on a shelf from which it had been taken at the beginning.

In preparing for the film Snow discovered that the audio changes were more pronounced than the visual ones. To tie them together and make them equivalent he instructed the lab to exaggerate the light and dark in printing and also used a B roll which variously moved from normal to black to light to overexposure. Then toward the end of the film he split his single system out of phase using the B roll. Up to this point sound and light variations have been locked together in accordance with changes in camera speed. The film thus becomes descriptive of the sync

83

potentials of a single system audio-visual recording technique. Instead of making use of synchronization in its assumed and purely naturalistic manner, Snow has used the technology literally to abstract in sync.

From his New York loft Snow made a tape of dripping water mingled with street sounds which was later played on WBAI Radio. Subsequently Wieland proposed that they film *Dripping Water*. The sound of the water is at times synchronous with the visual drip and at other times not, and this vacillation draws the viewer's attention more closely to the image. Shot in medium close-up, water drips into a dish, a section of which is off-screen and is the apparent source of the water's escape, for throughout the ten-and-a-half minute film the water level remains the same. The camera is fixed, never moving to reveal the source of the water nor its escape nor the origin of the street sounds. One becomes acutely aware of these audio and visual presences both on- and off-screen, as framing is emphasized by what is included as well as omitted.

Snow refers to the eight-minute *Standard Time* as his "home, wife, camera, radio, turtle movie."[4] It is another example of the use in his art of family and surroundings in a manner dramatically different from the way Brakhage uses his. *Standard Time* was shot following *Wavelength* in 1967. It was done as a study-experiment and test for $\longleftrightarrow$; it now exists as a work on its own, though one can't avoid thinking of it in conjunction with $\longleftrightarrow$. It also has shades of *La Région Centrale* with adumbrations of the sound concerns at the heart of *"Rameau's Nephew"*... *Standard Time* consists of 360-degree and shorter pans. In the same *Cooperative Catalogue* description quoted above, he refers to it as having "circular and arc saccades and glances. Spacial [*sic*] and parallel sound."

In a brief section, the shorter movements are vertical as the camera tilts down recording the base of the tripod and up across a bed to the ceiling. A cat is seen and appears again a number of times. A turtle disappears under the bed. The camera passes a woman lying on the bed, later glances across her moving figure, and still later steals a glimpse of her naked body. The camera continually pans over an AM-FM tuner; it's prominence is mildly deceptive as one tends to look for some sync or other form of corresponding audio-visual system connected to it. Sometimes the volume becomes louder the nearer the camera is to the tuner, yet this is not consistent. The audio and visual lines are separate but related, sometimes functioning analogously as "eye space" and "ear space," as Snow captioned the two in conversation. Although the perceiver is centred in the space, sharing the

39. *Breakfast*
Photo: Michael Snow

camera's position and point of view, there is never a complete and comfortable spatial orientation. The panning proceeds at various speeds, becoming faster, abstracting the space and making it difficult to focus, slowing down, pulling suddenly and erratically shifting directions. The camera pauses briefly only a few times. Through most of the film a radio discussion about dance is heard and while the program and voices are unchanged, the volume goes up and down as the ear catches and focuses on words in a way not unrelated to what the eye is doing with the moving image. One of the participants says, "I try to look at the audience as a mass. I try not to distinguish any faces so that my concentration . . ." as the sound trails off. In one segment the film cuts abruptly at the end of a short pan on a small space, repeating the pattern over and over again, as the sound cuts synchronously with the visual breaks. Near the end one hears the sound of a moving radio dial. Now very much in unison, the camera pans round and round quickly as the dial surveys the range of programming across the radio band.

40. *Breakfast*
Photo: Michael Snow

It is clear that after completing *Wavelength* Snow had immediately pursued his camera investigations in another area. *Standard Time* is a small exploration in pans and tilts of events within movement, the whole work in a sense almost exclusively representing a transition from one instant in time and place to another. This film suggests some of the abstraction possible from a moving camera, but the technique is more fully examined and systematically organized in ⟷ which followed.

Snow shot the fifteen-minute *Breakfast,* a.k.a. *Table Top Dolly,* in 1972, put it aside and completed it in 1976. With humour the two titles together describe the film technically and in terms of content. *Breakfast* supplies the one movement which till now had been missing from Snow's body of films concerned with camera movement and also complements *Wavelength.* The movement of the zoom lens in *Wavelength* slowly, effortlessly shifts screen space for us, gradually metamorphosing the space before our eyes. In *Breakfast* we may at first be disconcerted by the camera which slowly comes toward the odd arrangement of breakfast foods on the table and which finally proves to be actually mounted on the table top in a dolly shot.

After the four major films (*Wavelength,* ⟷ , *La Région Centrale* and *"Rameau's Nephew"*. . .), *Breakfast* enters as comic relief. It is a kind of comedy without characters, where objects are taken over by the camera's actions. Accompanied by the sounds of dishwashing and sometimes a radio, the camera slowly moves into space. A clear plexiglass sheet was mounted in front of the camera before shooting. Because the plastic is totally transparent, as the camera edges forward across the blue-checkered table cloth the objects comically and mysteriously begin to slip and fall in front of it. The orange juice cartons, paper cups, Jersey Lu egg carton, butter, a plate of rolls, bend over and down; the cloth is crumpled; the foods and other items are squeezed together and a brown rectangular object seems to float or hang in the lower part of the screen against the plexiglass. The moving camera stops as the items are momentarily held, as if frozen in space. Then it quickly pulls out, displaying the table on which the dolly is being executed, in again and out as the film ends.

Breakfast has a further comic value. It comes as a break from the seriousness and growing academicism of certain film directions from the mid-sixties onward which emphasized self-questioning, exploring or examining, among other things, the fixed and moving camera. By 1976 such approaches had exhausted themselves although there were those who insisted on continuing. On one level *Breakfast* literally drives the problem into the wall. On an entirely differently level it is descriptive, mundane and almost sacrilegious after Brakhage's romantic ritualizations of the everyday.

The descriptive and the literal are recurring elements in Snow's work. In his and in related contemporary art, literalization and description have to do with a different attitude toward imagination and expression than is present in traditional realist or in highly symbolic and metaphoric art. In traditional realistic art description and literalization may be used as tools to naturalize spaces and viewers' attitudes toward those spaces, whereas a literal and descriptive art such as Snow's employs reality to work against naturalization and a transparency and to call these assumptions into question.

Particularly since 1969 Snow has made a significant number of film, photographic and sound works which use immediacy and description. Chapter 3 dealt with examples among his photographic works. Description and literalization, which sometimes work together, are manifested in several ways. A title may name the activity in a piece *(Dripping Water)* or the objects involved. But quite apart from titles, works like *Dripping Water* and *Log* (1973-74) directly describe themselves visually. Still others are described both verbally and visually, as in *A Casing Shelved* (1970). The description may refer to the process of making, as in *Two Sides to Every Story,* or it may simply explain what the objects are and how they have functioned, as in a section of *"Rameau's Nephew". . . ,* where a voice-over narrates the movement of objects on a table (see chapter 8).

Puns are a favourite device of Snow's and an important aspect of his literalisms and descriptions. *Table Top Dolly, Press* and *Venetian Blind* are three such examples. *Hearing Aid* (1976) is a sound work using portable cassette recorders and a metronome. And in *"Rameau's Nephew". . .* the *sink/sync* sound section is untitled. In the course of describing and explaining this section, one inevitably puns on it.

Another work existing in two versions, both from 1970, is actually named *Sink.* One, of which there are three copies, consists of a 10" x 12" colour photograph seen under "normal" lighting. The other *Sink* consists of two parts—a 10" x 12" colour photograph and 100 35mm slides of the sink, all taken from the same fixed camera position. The photograph is mounted on the wall next to the series of projected slides. For the slides the sink was lit from the side, with coloured gels or transparencies placed over the lights and not over the camera lens when shooting. Variations of hue and tone affect the depth of field of the slides as

41. *Sink*
Photo: Michael Snow

the viewer measures their differences against the adjacent photo-graph, which acts as a constant index, and then compares the slides, each successive one against those now gone and in memory. While tinting film, slide or photographic images with gels and transparencies is a frequent practice of Snow's, most notably in *Wavelength,* it should be emphasized that in *Sink* Snow is working with gels to colour the light rather than for the different effect achieved by placing them directly over the lens.

Some of the very transparencies from *Wavelength* have found their way into *Sink.* The sink represented is the one in Snow's former studio on Canal Street in New York where *Wavelength* was made.[5] Apart from these somewhat subtle references, autobiography is implied here in a more obvious manner. Brushes, a tube of paint, an ink bottle, paper cup, rags and rings of paint stain in and on the sink all point to Snow's previous activity as painter.[6] Both versions might be called *Artist's Sink,* to be more literally descriptive. About the projected version Snow has commented: "You have to see the whole sequence in order to see the range of the kinds of realities involved in actually lighting the sink....I worked with coloured light to make coloured light."[7]

88

Titles seem only partially to describe as in *Sink* and *Tap*. But the combination of verbal and visual description can alter information as occurs for example in *Side Seat* where one has no real sense of the paintings from the side seat view and, in different ways, in *A Casing Shelved* and in *Two Sides to Every Story*.

Snow called his 1969 *Tap* "a kind of still sound movie,"[8] but in that direction, even more appropriate is Pierre Théberge's reference to *A Casing Shelved* as "a talking picture."[9] Like *Sink, A Casing Shelved* also exists in two versions: a 35mm colour slide with audiotape; and, in three copies, a 13½" x 10½" colour photograph with a cassette tape and player. Théberge's comment applies to the slide and tape. On magnetic tape Snow describes a blue wooden bookcase and its contents. The case has turned repository for materials involved in various of his art-making projects over the years. Contents are named and described for the eye and categorized according to apparent shape (such as lines, cylinders, spheres, rectangles), colour, kind of material and mundane function; but they are also named and described for the mind and memory according to their history and "significance" in Snow's life as artist. The significances and descriptive histories extend past the shelves, encroaching on the surrounding studio and even the space beyond. For instance, he notes on the tape that the packaging on one of the shelves contains coloured transparencies used in *Wavelength* and *Sink;* the green rubber ball is from ⟵——⟶ and is the only sphere present; on the left side, second shelf from the top hangs a calendar from 1962 or 1963 with the Walking Woman on it; *Authorization* was made with the Polaroid camera on the left; and the blue shelving or bookcase is the one which appeared in *Wavelength,* shot in that same Canal Street studio in 1966. Here language is employed in reference partly to what the eye can actually see and partly to more than can be known through sight, as Snow now constructs from these objects and memories in his detached autobiographical description another and separate work of art.

Two Sides to Every Story (1974) is Snow's only installation film work. Its very nature makes it impossible to assimilate all the given audio and visual information in any one particular moment. Like *Crouch, Leap, Land,* for which the viewing is isomorphic with its production, here the actual projection situation is isomorphic with its making. Snow employs literalism and description in the title as well as visually and in part verbally through his directions on the sound track. With their mechanisms synchronized, two stationary cameras mounted on tripods were set up facing each other approximately forty feet apart. On one side of a room, backed by a white wall, Snow sits in a director's chair next to a cameraman peering through his viewfinder. Across the room, backed by a window, the second cameraman records the space and activity going on in front of him as synchronously he is being recorded by the camera opposite. A constant rainfall is heard while the first camera films the dark window with its moving traffic lights and reflections from the outside beyond the second cameraman, who continues to record the opposite view which includes Snow, script in hand, directing a walking woman. Her movements, back and forth, are recorded by both cameras, front and back. When the work is installed, two projectors at opposite walls are run synchronously corresponding to the shooting situation; a thin plane is suspended in the centre of the space, each side a screen for the respective projections. An analogue to the physical projection plane exists in the filming procedure as Snow carries the transfer from making to viewing one literal step further, emphasizing in the course of it, dually, the space of the real plane as well as the space of the imaginative or fictional plane. He instructs the woman to walk to the centre of the space. As she presses her hands forward one notices a thin transparent hanging sheet; she is handed an aerosol can and sprays it green with a circular motion. A man slits the sheet from the other side and she passes through. Soon she is equipped with a mat board, blue on one side and yellow on the other, and the cameramen are given blue and yellow transparencies. At Snow's various instructions, the screen may become a plane of solid colour on one side, while on the other the woman may be seen from the rear with only edges of the mat board visible, or one or another screen may be tinted. The visual dialogue between cameras continues to record their respective fields of action. But the viewer receives only partial information, hearing one instruction which is actualized on the other side and having to walk about continually to take in the whole. Snow's instructions are also descriptions of actions, moments in time and light, colour changes, and demonstrations of the screen's two- and three-dimensional range of illusions.

The physical plane of projection serves as an analogue for the shooting plane and in turn as an analogue for the space of the imagination and the plane of the imaginary and fictional. While the green-sprayed plastic sheet is cut during shooting and then disappears, it is metaphorically transferred to the projection plane as later we see the woman return to the centre and extend her hands as if pressing, thereby gesturally remaking the surface. That transparent, then partially painted, plane which is destroyed in the filmmaking process is figuratively recreated in the suspended plane of projection, which becomes both a pun on and

42. *Two Sides to Every Story*
Photo: The National Gallery of Canada

a metaphor for the Coleridgean "suspension of disbelief" and the prerequisite for our poetic faith in the imaginary and fictional events which follow. In Snow's piece, both camera and plane serve as synonyms for imagination. The illusion is projected onto the real plane. The fabrication of one camera is revealed by the other, round and round, back and forth, on the plane. But as we see it, the imaginary becomes real. Though we know the truth, we believe the lie and espouse it. One embraces and balances the other. As early on in the film the transparency is destroyed but exists and continues figuratively, so also are the imaginary, illusory and fictional not destroyed but supported by the revealing powers of the camera projected onto the plane.[10]

In book form *Cover to Cover,* published in 1976, in many ways parallels and complements *Two Sides to Every Story.* In *Two Sides* the director plays himself. *Cover to Cover* is the result of another distanced use of self in the course of art-making. Here

91

43. *Cover to Cover*
Photo: T.E. Moore, Isaacs Gallery

Snow is subject/participant as he and his actions are observed and analyzed by two 35mm still cameras. If *Two Sides* brings to mind the nineteeth-century photographer Edweard Muybridge's use of two and three still cameras to record front, back and/or side of his serialized studies of animal and human locomotion, *Cover to Cover* is even more strongly reminiscent. Like Muybridge's series and Snow's *Two Sides, Cover to Cover* is analytical in the way it is structured and executed. As in the two-screen film, each double-take is printed recto-verso, although at times opposite sides appear next to each other on an open double page. It is a text of photographs which, like so many of Snow's works, reveals the process involved. There are illusions and illusions of illusions. Snow is subject observed in the book at the same time that he is reader reading and artist choosing and making decisions about images.

Cover to Cover, in 360 pages, becomes a full circle. One follows Snow from his house to his car to his gallery where a Walking Woman stands and where he examines a copy of the completed *Cover to Cover* and returns home. As one opens the front cover, Snow is seen entering the door, and the text ends with the artist holding up and having photographed the photographs of both sides of the door. The other side of the door

92

appears on the back cover. The book is designed so that it can be read front to back or back to front and in such a way that the reader must turn it around at the centre to carry on.

Words appear as credits on the back of a photograph (of a cameraman with tripoded camera) inserted into a typewriter. The few words in the text and other signs which exist, such as a traffic signal, are incorporated into images. *Cover to Cover* is a silent text in which images are equivalent to a written text. The equation is strengthened by the suggested parallel between camera and typewriter. One puts a page into a typewriter upside down and pulls it through right side up as one types on it. Analogous to the retina of the eye, the camera registers an image upside down on emulsified paper. Camera and typewriter each deal with signs and languages manifested in their own ways.

The book documents while it also fabricates the fiction. It narrates but it also pauses to analyze images more extensively— close-up, medium shots, top and bottom as well as sides, front and back. It abstracts spaces. As it documents, *Cover to Cover* also points, often with humour, to some of the fictions it is creating, such as Snow's van falling off a page or the bottom side of an LP shot as if on a turntable. The document of Snow making the book and the book within the book come full circle. The book is made and the fiction is created. They are one and same enclosed cover to cover.[11]

Snow employs techniques and devices of description and literalization to undercut conventional realism and audience involvement so often taken for granted in the highly illusionistic reproductive media in which he works. Descriptive title, visual or verbal information about the work, its materials and processes operate as devices to double[12] or reiterate the object's or event's presence in another state or to dissect object or event. And Snow's use of autobiography and the everyday, aided by his camera techniques, instead of maximizing involvement also distance the viewer.

Chapter 6

Teaching Space: ←——→

44, 45. ←——→
Photos: The National Gallery of Canada

←——→ is Snow's second major film. It highlights that "realism of process" first referred to in conjunction with *Lac Clair* as well as the photographic works and the more recent *Two Sides to Every Story*. It may include making or perceiving or both. In ←——→ realism of process works closely together with literalism, description and doubling and at times it is difficult to distinguish and separate their operations.

In the course of producing it, Snow described ←——→, contrasting it to *Wavelength*. "In the new film I am thinking about some sort of different orientation or emphasis that the spectator has, some kind of different participation. The new one is more objective, I think, than *Wavelength* and it involves you in some way which I don't know how to describe—exactly what your eyes and mind are doing when you're watching that."[1] ←——→ is more objective than *Wavelength*. Like the three shorter films discussed earlier which were made with a nonmoving camera, ←——→ exists on the surface. But it has a particular kind of surface quality. Its pictographic title describes its horizontal movement. Keeping in mind Snow's own comparison of these two long films, one realizes how truly literal ←——→ is measured against the earlier work. Yet perhaps because of its literalisms and use of description together with realism of process, ←——→ raises other issues.

In July 1968 Snow participated in a seminar at Fairleigh Dickinson University in Madison, New Jersey. He chose to shoot ←——→ in a relatively new prefabricated classroom on the suburban campus. Alan Kaprow, Max Neuhaus and other artists were there at the time and appear in the work. ←——→ was filmed on and off over a two-week period, with the beginning shot at about ten or eleven o'clock in the morning, the middle at about noon or one o'clock and the tilting section at about three or four o'clock in the afternoon. Unlike *Wavelength,* which was done on various stocks, here a single type of fast and granular film was used. There were no filters, and a wide-angle lens with a normal light exposure was employed. Thus colour changes are the result of the various speeds of the movement of tilting and panning, a few adjustments in the camera's shooting speed combined with alterations in natural and artificial light in and outside of the classroom—and the often abrupt and unexpected staccato cuts which create afterimages.

Some of the beginning of the film is loop printed. Overall, *One Second in Montreal* and ←——→ are the most systematic of Snow's films. The two are frequently shown together, *One Second in Montreal* following ←——→, eliciting strange psychological and physiological reactions. For ←——→ Snow wrote out speeds with a metronome. He had devised a machine for the camera action which would manipulate the speed of panning and permit the camera to move very rapidly, but in the end it proved not totally successful and Snow had to execute two-thirds of the movements by hand. The tripod was equipped with a wooden arm at each extreme of the camera's designated panning length, measuring the pan and acting as a stop device. Snow's prescoring and planned equipment were precursors of his *La Région Centrale* machinery (now adapted as a video work in *De La*). The audio proved difficult. Two principal sounds are heard throughout—a machine in the background and wood clapping in synchronization with the camera movement. But this was post-synced, both sounds in fact manufactured after the film was shot and edited. To make the in-sync clapping effect, Snow notched black leader measured to the movements and played this on a projector while he recorded it in conjunction with the sound of a motor equipped with a rheostat. He completed editing and sound recording and ←——→ was finished in January 1969.

The classroom location fits clearly and obviously into the literalizations with which Snow is involved. While Hollis Frampton, conveniently enough interviewed by Michael Snow, had spoken of his own films in part as "an effort to reconstruct the history of films as it should have been,"[2] Snow had already made ←——→, one of the parts of his systematic exploration of the camera. ←——→ literally presents itself as didactic; as Snow says: "It is in/of/depicts a classroom."[3] As it had never been done before, Snow is investigating the parameters of velocity for the panning and tilting camera and how the image is affected by time, speed, space and light.

If one sometimes forgets that the zoom in *Wavelength* is constantly changing the frame, eliminating the space and altering perspective, in ←——→ one is unavoidably conscious of the panning of the camera. There is absolutely no stasis in ←——→, signaled from the very beginning as the film opens on the outside of a classroom in the obviously suburban campus setting and the camera picks up a man walking by. After a brief solid green image-field the film cuts to the inside of the room. The panning camera was positioned to shoot from the right side and corner of the room at an angle to the windowed wall, embracing an approximately 100-degree visual field. Four double windows are distinctly separated, two on each side, by a thin plaster column extending from the wall. A door, on the wall at a diagonal to the shooting camera, leads outside into a road and walkway. Houses, grass and trees are seen through the windows and open door. The windowed wall and door are most prominent on screen. A chalkboard, movable student desks and above them fluorescent lights which are turned on and off are seen on screen left.

As the film proceeds with its panning at a moderately fast speed, the column in the centre of the wall seems to bend as do the windows, especially those on the left. After several minutes a figure enters the frame and is seen on the outside of the classroom taking off storm windows, first one on the right and then on the left. The same man cleans several windows, spraying and wiping them with up and down and back and forth movements. More activities follow: another man sweeps out the doorway with a push broom; a girl sits at a desk shaking her long hair, implying yes or no, as a man writes on the board; a figure seems barely to straddle the right side of the frame and then vanishes midway; throughout the film figures are abruptly cut from frame in staccato fashion as the camera continues back and forth; a man and a woman play catch; a car goes by right; a girl standing at a window on the right reading a book pops out of frame, reappears on the left, is joined by a man as they talk, embrace and are quickly gone; another woman at a desk recites "back and forth, to and fro, hither and yon, hither and thither," disappears, edited out of frame; a class watches a man draw the double arrow on the board; a perambulatory figure pops out on reaching the last window pane on the right; a class sits conversing inaudibly; a group of people stand around in what appears a social gathering, two among them staging a fist fight, and a short while later— about a third of the way through the film—the party vanishes. Other action occurs, such as people and cars moving past.

Meanwhile, throughout these activities the speed of the panning has slowed down, reaching perhaps its slowest point at the fight, and then has increased considerably after the party scene. At times the grain is pronounced and colours shift from pinks to blues to greens to cold steel shades, and lines and shadows appear and disappear. On the moderately fast stroboscopic speeds one has difficulty adjusting one's focus. Throughout the viewer must work actively to remain with the images and to follow the transformations of the film on the screen. At faster speeds the frame seems to expand almost to a cinemascopic size, creating an illusion of a sliding back and forth horizontal extension or elongation. In film terms, this part of ←——→ reminds one of

46. ⟵———⟶
Photo: The National Gallery of Canada

Michael Fried's notion of deductive structure in painting when he spoke of Frank Stella "deriving or deducing pictorial structure from the literal character of the picture-support" and answering the internal needs and logic of the painterly problems he was dealing with in his significant and influential shaped canvases.[4] While Stella's is an actual physical change, Snow uses optical illusions virtually to alter the screen size for the perceiver. But then as panning speed greatly increases, instead of an illusion of screen extension, one picture seems to displace another, back and forth, and the sound now suggests a compatible effect of slides clicking in and out of place in a carrousel machine. As panning accelerates the image becomes blurred and abstracted. One colour is transformed into another before the viewer realizes when or how the change has occurred. At a very fast speed the combined image-sound creates a highly illusionistic experience with the sensation, for instance, of looking out the window of a moving train or of standing in a station watching a fast train pass by; it appears that one can see more of the outside of the room and beyond in this abstracted section than earlier and it also becomes somewhat less difficult to adjust one's focus. The sound enforces the train-like illusion. The space pops back and forth along the screen.

At the moment of most intense and relentless speed and abstraction, the film cuts from the horizontal to the vertical. The movement appears even faster now, the imagery more abstract and seemingly without connection to the previous two-thirds of the film. This change comes as a surprise, less because of the shift from pan to tilt than from the sudden appearance of a visually unidentifiable abstraction, which is generically unrelated to what has gone before. The linking element seems to be the nature of the movement. From salmon-pink and blue the image gradually shifts its hues to blues, greens, dark brown and black sections as the speed gradually slows down. Streaked and gridded areas of the picture are revealed to be the pattern of the cover on the fluorescent light as the camera passes from the ceiling light fixture, which is now seen to have a strip of black masking tape on it, past the window down to another black tape mark on the floor. A car is heard pulling up and a policeman appears at one of the windows, stares inside and then leaves. Credits appear, but the film isn't over, as Snow follows with a coda recapitulating ⟵———⟶ in superimposition from various parts of the film. Horizontal and vertical, right side up and upside down, the speeds, colours, light qualities, ambient sounds out of sync as well as a section of silence are all to be compared here and now, measures of memory. Clapping accompanies a solid green image-field as the film ends.

In serving analogously as a mnemonic device, the coda points to the difficulty of recalling which of the human and mechanical events and the light and speed of movement changes occur precisely when in ←——→. While the human events have been listed above in the succession in which they happen, there is nothing which dictates any order for them or causes one to remember them in this way, except perhaps for the entry and exit of the policeman.

As in the case of *Wavelength,* an absolutely accurate description of ←——→ measured precisely in feet and minutes will not be synonymous with a phenomenological one. But phenomenologically the experience of the one film is strikingly different from the other. The camera concentrates and frames attention in *Wavelength,* moving in and eliminating more and more of the space of the room as it gradually brings into focus the photograph of ocean waves on the wall which finally fills the screen. Through the vehicle of the camera the perceiver seems to enter into the experience of the film. But in ←——→ , as Snow remarked, "You aren't within it, it isn't within you, you're beside it."[5] One is "beside" the constant movement of the film. Visually and perceptually it does not invite ingress or access into it. Elsewhere Snow wrote: "The film is really relationships—reciprocity. There's a teacher and students, lovers—the whole thing is action and reaction. Two people toss a ball. And somehow or other the cop enters into that."[6] The reciprocity exists on and across the screen. Events, situations and movements answer and fulfill each other as the perceiver remains beside them. The horizontal and the vertical movements are the film's armature and like the zoom of *Wavelength* become forms of seriality, and the other actions and gestures become series and variations within its theme. And this analysis begins to imply why one remains beside it: each reciprocity, as it fills in, becomes self-contained, and one reads the double-headed arrow and its orchestration of related movements as constructing an object in and of itself. Snow said that he had thought of titling it with a pair of bisecting double-headed arrows (←—✝—→) which would have been even more literal but would have eliminated the surprise shift to the vertical movement.

Thus one can read ←——→ in its descriptiveness as enclosed—literally self-referential, as it seems to prohibit involvement by its very structure. While the film keeps the viewer beside it, its very physical controlling quality and resulting shape is nonetheless demanding in how and why it does this. For it shuts one out and distances one, consciously manipulating perceptually, often eliciting physiological reactions of genuine discomfort, sometimes joined to anger and/or irritation. (Perhaps the clapping on the sound tract at the end is a bit of black humour on Snow's part.) But in keeping the viewer out and simultaneously creating a kind of object of film sculpture, ←——→ spills over into metaphor and like *Wavelength,* demands further readings. Paradoxially, the very signs of its self-containment, its fulfilling reciprocity, force the film out of itself and elicit other meanings.

Snow refers to ←——→ as physics.[7] It is about velocity, and there is no stasis. It is a 100 percent moving image picture, an action movie. As an action picture its themes and variations on action and reciprocity imply the vignettes and tableaux of conventional fictional and dramatic movies which are themselves literalized into stereotypes: love, a fight, the law. Then there is another realm of reference to conventional film subjects: instruction, a class and a classroom setting—all suggesting the educational film—combined in a tertiary way with the presence of the social gathering along with the ordinary actions and attentions to the room such as sweeping, putting in storm windows and cleaning windows. One might consider these as documentary events.

But in suggesting conventional motifs of the fictional and dramatic action film in this didactic setting, ←——→ is in its own way commenting on the manipulations of that kind of cinema as well as other kinds of standard movie genres. Through its prime formal device of the panning camera it takes the ordinarily accepted and acknowledged content and shapes that into its overall back-and-forth, to-and-fro structure. The film manipulates perceptually and involves one physically, at the same time that it gives one distance beside the object. Thus, paradoxically, the viewer is not manipulated in the ordinary manner of the commercial narrative and even, and perhaps especially, the educational, instructional film. ←——→ establishes the conditions for reflectiveness while it also throws light, through its metaphors and setting, on those ways in which one acquiesces or unwittingly allows one's self to be taken in by conventions.

But in addition there are other levels of action and reaction or reciprocal completion which are more subtle and abstracted variations on back and forth. During an extremely fast section a man walks in and disappears, passing against the movement and tension of the camera. Later a woman, whose steps are also heard as were the man's, now leaves the room quickly with a push from the pan in contrast to the camera's pull against the man. Centred

100

between this push-pull of opposite movements and directions, a piece of paper appears on the wall briefly and then is gone. After the woman recites synonyms for back and forth, another voice trailing off into inaudibility says: "There will always be action and reaction." A man refereeing the fist fight says: "It's pretty hard to come to a decision. I call it a draw." There are numerous other examples, many suggested in the description above. But more abstractly, while the camera is positioned asymmetrically to the windowed wall, the column which bisects the wall serves to accentuate what are two dramatically distinct spaces, because the interior and exterior light combined with changing shooting speeds and camera movement at times vary colours and illusions on the respective sides of the space. And the film begins outside of a room which is also outdoors and then picks up inside of the same room while the coda brings together inside and outside, upside up and upside down, horizontal and vertical, sound and silence.

Realism of process returns this time under the aegis of manipulation, a complicated issue in ⟵———⟶ which itself needs further discussion. While the panning and tilting movement becomes highly controlling of the viewer perceptually, because of the hyperbolization of movement one remains aware that one is being manipulated. It is this consciousness, for one thing, which distinguishes ⟵———⟶ from a dramatic action film whose techniques and motifs are designed to go unnoticed in order to heighten transparency and the viewer's suspension of disbelief. But here one is distanced.

One can trace analogues for dramatic action through the fragments of plot motifs but also through the serial-like panning and tilting movements. The moving camera becomes the vehicle and mechanical surrogate for dramatic action. In a dramatic or fictional film there is a point where one begins to expect a relief or resolution. In ⟵———⟶ one comes to anticipate a physical relief, but instead of providing this Snow alters the direction and even increases the speed of movement. This change is totally unanticipated, for until now the viewer has been completely aware of the manipulations though also experiencing the building tension. There has been no deception with the clear, literal surface of exterior manipulation which reveals itself as it proceeds and unfolds with the abstractions and range of illusions which occur on the screen. Here realism of process takes place on the levels of making and perceiving.

But then instead of winding down and reaching a resolution, the movement changes directions and accelerates, increasing tension. At this point the image appears totally abstracted and

101

completely unrelated to the previous two-thirds of the film. Realism of process, the concrete/abstract, the literal all seem lost, for the procedures and materials of image-making are no longer clear and apparent. The viewer may now begin to feel controlled by the unidentifiable abstraction as well as the abrupt change in direction combined with continued speed of movement. The tension of this unanticipated movement and speed created purely through the technology and materials of film sustain the analogue of dramatic tension. The velocity and the now foreign image-abstraction become wholly manipulative in the same manner as are the ploys and techniques of the highly illusionistic fiction and dramatic film, for in both cases the means are hidden.

In striking contrast to the previous purely physical and perceptual maneuvers in ⟷, this action neither allows the elements concerned to be identified nor brings about a consciousness of the process involved in the making of it. But finally this section proves to be the complement of the panning camera as the tilting camera gradually decelerates and one begins to recognize the representation out of which the abstraction has been made—and realism of process has not been lost or destroyed. The dramatic analogue, moreover, is continued: one sees the tilting section progressively slow down and in doing so unravel the mystery of its initial abstraction. It becomes a denouement, or more literally a falling action, and as it slows down one thinks back over the structure of Snow's film. A linear ordering unfolds and one sees ⟶ make formal use of the basic pattern of the dramatic action film. There is the exposition or introduction of events, including most of the human motifs and mechanical activities which occur in the first third of the film. The speed of panning goes from medium fast to very slow at the party to its slowest during the fist fight. Rising action follows as the panning accelerates and comes to its climax, cuts to rapid tilting, and then to the falling action or denoue-ment.[8] The slowing down within itself might be looked at also as a physical relief. And in another analogue of the drama, the disguised or unidentified image is now revealed and resolved. The policeman arriving, staring into the window and "casing the place," as Manny Farber put it,[9] and then leaving, offers several quite varied dramatic and other readings. His presence is ambiguous and provides a loose thread for the construction of a narrative out of preceding events. For another perceiver he might appear as a deus ex machina, signaling that order has been restored and that all is under control. For some he may reflect mystery or threat or prohibition, for others a welcome comic relief. But on top of these dramatic readings the policeman is also looking out and through the window at us, the viewers, as the window metaphor is literally reversed in a self-referential gesture.

If one looks at ←——————→ as an analogue of dramatic structure from exposition through denouement, the film's panning through tilting loosely assumes a linearity in the sense that it is necessary for the viewer to follow from the beginning in order to participate in the realism of the process of perception. But the realism of process—and the very shape of the film—is actually generated out of the film materials themselves: movement of the camera, adjusted speeds of shooting, kind of film stock and the nature of the altered light. With different speeds of movement the images themselves change as ←——————→ reveals its self-evident conjuring and its range of illusion and abstraction. One is reminded of how Georges Méliès as a nineteenth-century magician had to hide the sources of his trickeries, though he announced his films as "trick films," while Snow in contrast reveals them, keeping nothing from his viewers.

Through literalism and description ←——————→ points to itself and its surface qualities. Yet its very terms refer to and give rise to metaphors about conventions within the larger tradition of film history. Through what seem to be limited and minimal means of exploration in *Wavelength* and ←——————→ , Snow creates discontinuities out of accepted givens and lays bare his means of making. The former film is about more than a zooming camera and the latter more than panning and tilting. In its didactic setting, ←——————→ questions assumptions about the manipulations and mechanizations of the dramatic film, and by literalizing its means, suggests parallels to that dramatic structure. While ←——————→ is very much concerned with surface, literalization and description engender ideas and perceptions outside of its surface and because of this same surface.

One can begin to see now how Snow's use of exploration and analysis, description, literalization and realism of process, and his unique and anomalous kind of autobiography all relate to surfaces. His ideas and methods convey particular kinds of attitudes toward art-making as well as toward the objects or experiences produced. He moves away from obscure mythology and mythopoesis, atavistic psychological preoccupations and totally inscrutable expression and intention, directing the viewer's attention to the immediate hard and dry surface of the work of art in its clarity, legibility and accessibility. These devices of exploration and description particularly serve to separate the artist from the products of his labour as they also distance the perceiver from the work and its maker. As the viewer focuses attention on the surface of the work, the romantic mythology of the artist loses its significance and the artist's role in relationship to the task and end product is redefined. Such is the case in dealing with Snow and his art.

Echoing T. E. Hulme, who early in the century spoke out for a poetic language which was "hard and dry,"[10] Robbe-Grillet speaks of breaking away from a humanistic attitude and vocabulary to the "hard, dry objects which are behind them." His attitude toward objects and their surfaces, distance and description, is stated very succinctly:

To describe things, as a matter of fact, is deliberately to place oneself outside them, confronting them. It is no longer a matter of appropriating them to oneself, of projecting anything onto them. Posited, from the start, as *not being man,* they remain constantly out of reach and are, ultimately, neither comprehended in natural alliance nor recovered by suffering. To limit oneself to description is obviously to reject all the other modes of approaching the object: sympathy as unrealistic, tragedy as alienating, comprehension as answerable to the realm of science exclusively.[11]

These notions are clearly reflected in the works of Michael Snow discussed in this and previous chapters.

Chapter 7

De-Romanticizing Art and Artist:
La Région Centrale

As a move from ←——→ I decided to extend the machine aspect of film so that there might be a more objective feeling, you wouldn't be thinking of someone's expressive handling of the thing but perhaps how and why the whole thing got set in motion, what's behind it. In both ←——→ and La Région Centrale once it is set up it keeps on going.

Here Snow embraces the machine and its potential, adding, "I only looked in the camera once. The film was made by planning and by the machinery itself."[1] This seems a logical step after ←——→. Three years earlier Snow had remarked that he thought ←——→ more objective than *Wavelength*. Once again, as one might guess, Snow differs radically from Brakhage concerning the machine and self-expression.

In 1974 Brakhage completed his *Text of Light* and dedicated it to James Davis who, beginning in the 1940s, made films with refracted light. In *Text of Light* he makes use of an ashtray to create a seventy-minute display of refracted light in a wide spectrum of colours and tone values. Jonas Mekas, in his review of the film in the *Village Voice*, stresses the fact that Brakhage's film is "handmade" without the help of a Lumia or other light-manufacturing device. "Stan did it without any such machines. He beat the machine. And he did better than any machine will ever do: his work is richer in colour, and it has form and shape and rhythm. Once and for all Stan dismissed the machine as the creator: he, Stan, is the creator and machines are only means." Mekas concludes, "But then—who knows what the light is all about? The *Text of Light* is about the light of Stan Brakhage. I have my own light. And you have your own. But Stan's light text helps me to read my own light texts clearer and subtler. I can pray in Stan's Cathedral of Light."[2]

Text of Light is basically a romantic work and the information Mekas offers only heightens its romantic aura. Brakhage worked on it painstakingly for nearly two years. According to Mekas he actually broke his back in the course of filming the ashtray with his handheld camera. One never in fact sees the ashtray in the film. One only knows that an ashtray is being filmed because Mekas tells his readers so, quoting Brakhage on the subject in his *Village Voice* column. The angst involved in "creating" and the

47. Michael Snow on location for
La Région Centrale, 1970.
Photo: Michael Snow

stress on the handmade are what count for Mekas and obviously for Brakhage as well. But what does angst have to do with the film?

Text of Light, with all the encomiums about its being Brakhage's "masterpiece," is basically a nineteenth-century work and, in fact, a reactionary one. One might expect to find that Brakhage had moved beyond his earlier ideas about "closed eye vision," mythopoesis and paramyth. In his past works Brakhage attempted to overcome conventional illusion-making. In the course of employing unorthodox means of image-making, he was not concerned with revealing the processes and materials. With the exception of *Blue Moses* (1962) Brakhage made his viewer conscious of his method only occasionally and indirectly. His materials and means have always been at the service of his romantic vision, his goal to make his viewers lose themselves in his illusions and images. Consequently, his work as a whole is minimally reflexive. In retrospect Brakhage's work looks increasingly romantic and concerned only with offering alternative images. In 1955, even 1965, however, it was necessary to present images contrary to the expected and accepted way of making film. Work that broke down conventional filmic notions even if it disguised its means of facture was still considered avant-garde. But it has been more than twenty years since Brakhage made *The Wonder Ring,* and radical changes in attitude toward illusionism, art making and the artist have taken place. Today Brakhage's "Cathedral of Light" no longer accommodates the demands of a conscious, critical, scrutinizing art perceiver. It presents only an "escape" to the seductive trap of the artist's hermetically sealed romantic vision.

Brakhage's radically different approach to his art throws into relief Snow's anti-romantic stand, the dimensions and ramifications of his ideas and the way in which the information he provides about his films helps the viewer to understand his work. The structure of *Text of Light* as understood through the information Brakhage gives and Mekas interprets in a quintessentially romantic way is, in effect, the heart and soul of Stan Brakhage. One appears only an extension of the other.

The purely descriptive information about the shooting of the ashtray in *Text of Light* misleads the viewer to expect to see it at some point during the film. This knowledge thus works critically against the film and the viewer's aesthetic assessment of it. There are times, however, when descriptions about the making of a work and clues and hints in straightforward prose about the processes involved are not merely helpful to an understanding but essential to full cognitive grasp of a work's significance.

For instance, Brakhage's *Mothlight* can be appreciated as an abstract film. If the perceivers know, however, that it was made not with film or camera but from pieces of moth and foliage on mylar tape, they will interpret the images differently. There is also the historical significance of this laborious, year-long task. It was made in 1963 at a time when pop art was reacting to the extreme subjectivity of abstract expressionism—precisely the kind of activity in which Brakhage was indulging.

Similarly, Tony Conrad's *4 X Attack* (1973) can be considered in light of its formal and historical implications. Conrad speaks of the film as his "expressionistic" or "abstract expressionistic" statement. How he made it dictates how the viewer must look at it. He took fifty feet of 4X film stock into his darkroom, unrolled it, smashed it with a hammer, flashed it before light, gathered all the pieces together and developed them. He then proceeded laboriously to "reconstitute the film." Editing was not compositional but reconstitutional since Conrad had to fit the pieces back into their original places along the film strip. The film exists as an object to be handled and examined. Conrad has made prints of *4 X Attack* so that one can also see a projection of his expressionistic statement. Clearly the projection means nothing unless one knows how and why it was done.

107

4 X Attack must be looked at in relation to abstract expressionism in painting and to the film work of Brakhage, particularly *Mothlight*. Only then does it have significance as a parody of romanticism. And a large part of the parody is a play on the handmade. Conrad literalizes the idea of the handmade, and by carrying it to a logical extreme makes of it a mechanical function. He counters it by stressing a priori decision-making and chance. Conrad's *4 X Attack* is antithetical to the beautiful, craftsmanly and ineffable work of Brakhage. His film may appear ineffable but clearly is not when one understand its mode of fabrication and its historical and aesthetic comment.

Knowing how Brakhage filmed *Text of Light* only brings into question its form and heightens the romantic image of Brakhage as anguished nineteenth-century figure ready to sacrifice all and suffer any amount of pain for his art. But knowing how *4 X Attack, Mothlight* and *La Région Centrale* were executed considerably increases understanding of each work. The critique and parody of the handmade in *4 X Attack* and the use of the machine in *La Région Centrale* in their separate ways call attention to those aspects of romanticism which place a premium on creativity, beauty, the soul and self-expression. Both films question such values and their relevance to the work of art. The slight, fifty-foot *4X Attack* is an anomalous handmade film while *La Région Central* is a formidable machine-made landscape film which reveals no human figure and nothing man-made or man-imposed in the wilderness in which it was filmed except the occasional shadow of the camera and the mechanical device on which it is mounted. While Mekas was jubilant that Stan Brakhage could in his estimation tower over the attempts of machines, specifically light-producing machines, Snow was concerned with what the machine could do, its objectivity and its separation from man.

If *4X Attack* plays with the metaphor of the hand, *La Région Centrale* dispenses with it altogether. In planning for the film Snow had two principal needs: 1) the appropriate electronic apparatus and mechanical device for his camera capable of executing the movements he sought; and 2) a location suitable to his concerns with movement and space. He made sketches of what the machinery might look like, but the feat demanded the expertise of an engineer. Then in 1969 a filmmaker friend in Canada put Snow in contact with Montreal technician Pierre Abeloos. In approximately a year's time Abeloos developed the appropriate electronics and machinery. After innumerable trips into the wilds of Quebec, Snow was still unable to find the

48. *De La*. The camera mount for *La Région Centrale* later became part of a video installation. See n. 17 for description.
Photo: Ellis Kerr, The National Gallery of Canada

location he wanted. Parodoxically, he sought an area totally untouched by man and man-made devices—not even a telephone pole—yet a place which would be easily accessible by car for hauling the equipment and crew. After resorting to maps and aerial photographs, Snow finally discovered the place he was looking for by helicopter—a mountain top with stones, boulders, surrounding hills and mountains, overlooking a lake—about one hundred miles north of Sept-Iles in Quebec. Since the place had no name, Snow considered using another nonverbal title like ⟵──⟶. It was Joyce Wieland who saw the words "La Région Centrale" in a physics text in a Quebec City bookstore and suggested it to Snow as a possible title.[3]

Abeloos designed the mounting device according to Snow's specifications for movement in such a way that no part of the mount was filmed in the course of shooting, although at times its shadow was purposely recorded by the constantly moving

109

camera. Sets of axles on the machine mount permitted multiple kinds of movements simultaneously. Snow prescored the kind of camera movements he wanted to achieve. The options for movement were horizontal, vertical, rotational, zoom, and camera start, along with speed variables for each one. As Snow described the set up: "Pierre [Abeloos] worked out a system of supplying the orders to the machine to move in various patterns by means of sound tapes. Each direction has a different frequency of an electronic sine wave assigned to it. It makes up a layer of tones divided into five sections starting very high, about 10,000 cycles per second, down to about seventy cycles. The speed information is in terms of beats or pulses going from slow to fast.... The machine can be operated with a set of dials and switches."[4]

Snow was still preparing the sound tapes when circumstances forced him to begin shooting. Thus, although the entire film was prescored, part of it was made by sound tapes and part by dialing the direction and speed through remote control. Partially as a consequence, after editing his visuals Snow discarded his fragments of sync sound and remade the sound track as close to the original working sound as he could. The audio is generally in sync with the visuals, coding the movements, although at times it becomes approximate, at other times falls behind and as with *Side Seat Paintings Slides Sound Film,* at the end sound and visuals totally break apart.

In September 1970 Snow returned to the site by helicopter with Abeloos, Wieland and an assistant, assembled the machinery and electronic remote-control equipment, mounted the camera and remained for five days in the cold of the mountain top. In all, approximately six hours of film were shot, parts of which were second takes. Included in this six hours is a half-hour segment documenting the activity of the crew as they installed the machinery along with a demonstration of the movements of the camera and machine. Snow later decided to omit this half-hour "human" segment because he felt that it totally altered his original idea. Indeed it not only alters it but, in fact negates it.[5]

In the first of two articles on *La Région Centrale,* John W. Locke remarks that while it is a film of constant camera movement there is neither a tracking, a dolly nor a handheld camera shot.[6] In ←———→ the camera is mounted on a tripod and moves continually. In *Wavelength* only the zoom lens of the tripod-mounted camera moves. *La Région Centrale* incorporates both pans and zooms. Its mount acts as a tripod and at times as a kind of small crane enabling the camera attached to a shaft to move out from the centre of the base up to four feet in any direction—up, down, around, across. What results are combinations of movements which are unique to film. Snow remarks, "You see, the camera moves around an invisible point completely in 360 degrees, not only horizontally but in *every* direction and on every plane of a sphere. Not only does it move in predetermined orbits and spirals but it itself also turns, rolls and spins. So there are circles within circles and cycles within cycles. Eventually there's no gravity."[7] There are also figure-8s, arcs, scallops, sweeps, zigzags, horizontal shifts, Möbius strips, tipping and rocking of the image within the frame, along with a shaking effect and angling or tilting of the image in the frame. Several movements are possible simultaneously: the camera may pan horizontally and zoom with shifts upward, for example; or the image may turn in the frame while it is being zoomed in and out. Once a particular movement is executed over a period of time in a section, it is never precisely repeated; variations on it occur in conjunction with other movements, directions and/or speeds.

La Région Centrale begins with the sounds of its electronic tones, then a bright yellow X cuts across a dark screen. There are no titles nor are the sections numbered. There are, however, seventeen sections in the film, each separated by an X. For the sake of convenience I will refer to them here by number. Their length varies from as much as thirty minutes in sections 1 and 17 to three minutes in section 3 to the shortest, approximately thirty seconds, in section 13. The progression of its parts is loosely linear. *La Région Centrale* begins about noon-time, proceeds to mid-afternoon, continues from sunset to night to sunrise, and ends about noon.

Following the first X is a slow 360-degree pan around the rocky ground surrounding the machine-mounted camera. The panning continues and the camera begins a slight but regular upward shift which increases the circumference of its circle, as it gradually takes in more and more of its environment—small rocks, boulders, mountain sides, distant hills, a lake, and finally the sky. There are also frequent glimpses of the shadow of the camera and its moving machinery. The shifting ceases. Panning becomes faster now on the clear white or pale blue sky. The viewer is no longer aware of movement but only of the slightest change in colour. Yet one knows that there is movement because of the sine signals, just as one knows that the shifting upwards has resumed because of a corresponding sound. There is an abrupt cut from the light sky to the static yellow X which leaves its strong afterimage on the beginning of the next section. This section starts with fast panning in the sky, the environment is suddenly turned upside down, and then it begins to turn around in the

111

49, 50. *La Région Centrale*
Photos: The National Gallery of Canada

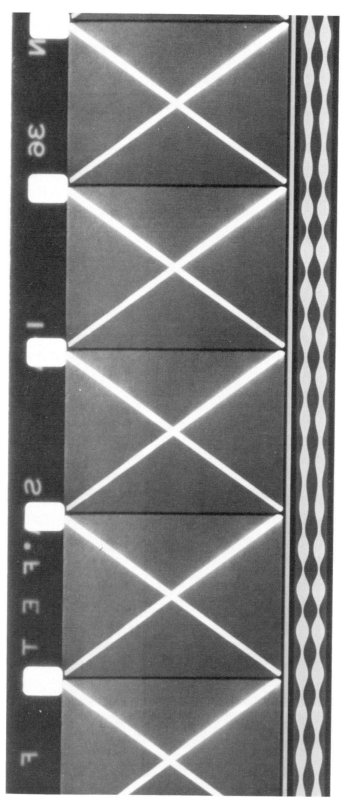

frame. This effect is produced by rotating the camera on its lens. These movements and the more or less synchronized corresponding electronic sounds occur very quickly. Suddenly the turning slows down and just as suddenly there is a cut to an X. The third short section consists of a sky to ground figure-8-like pattern which includes the shadow of the machine as the camera repeats the configuration over and over again.

The camera proceeds with movements "in *every* direction and on every plane of a sphere," if one can imagine the camera as cutting through the sphere. Besides the rotation of the camera on its lens, as in the second section in which most of the image rolls around a stable centre point, the camera itself also moves clockwise or counterclockwise, the whole image-field shifting around constantly from side to side of the frame. At other times, instead of sky-land moving clockwise or counterclockwise to the frame along the plane of the screen, the image seems to rotate outward from the screen, or the horizon shifts so that sky-land in its ordinary gravity-bound situation tilts to the vertical, moving by on the screen like a strip going up and around or down and around. Besides working off the trajectories of a sphere, the moving camera also plays itself off of the rectangle of the screen. For instance, in a shot in which the rotating screen image is dominated by sky passing clockwise or counterclockwise around a centre point, a piece of the land is triangulated into each screen corner successively as it disorients the viewer. With the screen filled mostly with sky, as the image revolves it may only slightly skirt a mountain top. The camera may skim the land, barely place it at the top of the frame, then shift it to one side, then across the bottom and so on. In this way Snow accepts and accentuates the tension between circle and rectangle.

In section 1 and several other times during the film, either when the camera is on a light sky or shooting in darkness, sound is one's only clue to movement. If one is not aware from the start how sound relates to movement one will register this correspondence only as the film progresses.

The sky itself plays a distinctive role in the film. The end of the opening section hints at this. But it is night in sections 9 and 10, dawn in section 11 and the noon sun of the end which underline this role. In section 9, after up-and-down pans between rocks and sky, the camera begins a zigzag pattern, moving around the landscape 360 degrees again and again. The screen becomes darker and darker, the sky streaked with lines of coloured light. Rocks and large boulders are silhouetted against the sky. This part ends with a panning sequence in virtual darkness, a preparation for section 10 in which the white moon is seen continuously arcing in and out from one corner, from another corner, then circling in the centre of the dark screen frame. The circling pattern is elongated to an oval one, and the moon leaves a comet-path afterimage. The movements of the white moon in the frame become faster and faster. An X appears. Section 11 begins on a dark blue sky with fast movements implied by the corresponding sound. Fairly rapidly the screen becomes light again, bringing in the dawn.

The night section, including sunset to sunrise, occurs approximately midway in the film. Similar to the first section which ends on a bright white screen, the sun-bleached frame of white light appears at the film's finale before the last X.

The 190-minute film proceeds without intermission. Asked about the length of *La Région Centrale,* Snow comments, "In seeing *One Second in Montreal* you have to be able to live with what is happening for a certain length of time in order to begin to understand it, to start to speculate with it. It is literally made with lengths of time. In a completely different way this applies to *La Région* too. It is a big space and it needed a big time. It's manageable however. Three hours isn't that long. You can see three hours."[8]

Given its length, its multipart composition structured without an intermission, the sound and the complexity of the camera movements, the task of describing *La Région Centrale* is radically different than it is for *Wavelength* and ←——————→. It has already been demonstrated that an absolutely accurate description of *Wavelength* or ←——————→ is not synonymous with a phenomenological one. A rather detailed chronology of events was given for ←——————→ in chapter 6, yet the viewer recalls very few of these in their correct order. Variations on action and reaction reinforce the panning and the overall central idea. In *Wavelength* one tends to recall the order of the human events because of implied causal relationships, but the other occurrences—light and colour changes and the moments of identification of the pictures on the wall—cannot be precisely registered and measured phenomenologically in the perceiver's time. *La Région Centrale,* however, presents other problems. One can describe the film in terms of its length, the number of its parts, its loosely linear progressions through day to night to day and its unity of time and place, along with a catalogue of types of movement and some of their combinations. It is useful to deal with certain parts more closely and precisely than others, yet a detailed description of all seventeen sections is unnecessary. Some of the movements almost defy verbal description because of what they do with angle and direction of compounded movements into and away from the screen surface. They must be seen as they visually describe themselves in space. This by no means suggests a romantic interpretation, but it does point to a different emphasis in the film. It is the large movements and the smaller variations of kinds of movements analyzing the landscape which have their cumulative effect over the more than three hours of film. Thus the focus of the film is not really each individual camera movement per se or each section, but the consequences of the kind of movement Snow has coded for his camera, the relationship between the orchestrated movements and the "big space" and the respective places of and relationships among the machine-mounted remote-control camera, landscape and viewer.

Devoid of all human presence, *La Région Centrale* shapes its own drama out of the conflict of the shape and the space of the recorded landscape conveyed through trajectories of movement at various speeds, by the clashes of the geometrics of circles, arcs and lines modelled by the camera against the rectangular screen and by contrasts of light and dark. Although section 9 ends in darkness, one does not expect the arcing and circling white moon of the following part. But this is the penultimate climax. The preparation for the climax is the accumulation of the lengths of time and variations of movement which precede the approximately thirty-minute final section. Within itself this section creates tensions in terms of speeds, directions of movement, and the rapport between the concrete and the abstract. After 360-degree panning on the distant horizon, the camera compounds the movements with a zoom-in, blurring rocks and boulders, then zooms out again. Following a rapid full-circle pan, the image turns around in frame, as its rotating movement goes from a slow lobbing effect, accelerating to a wobbling of the frame which carries with it the sensation of seasickness. The camera zooms out as the wobbling continues and one now glimpses for the last time the shadow of the machine. Without warning the fastest and most abstract passage in the film takes place as the camera sweeps from sky to land to sky to land, streaking the screen with browns and blues. This is faster even than the first part of the tilting in ←——→ . The speed is so great here that were sound-image synchronized, one might not be able to perceive it. The camera slows down to where the viewer can now reidentify ground and sky; it focuses on the white sky with its white sun where it appears to linger for a time.

There is no falling action here. The film simply stops. In contrast to the rising action, climax and falling action or unravelling in ←——→ , *La Région Centrale* has no such relationship in shape or form to the conventional dramatic action film and its deconstruction.

116

Just as the inchoate narrative in *Wavelength* and the conventional film motifs in ←——→ tend to dominate one's memory of the two films, so these dramatic moments of visual thematic climax stand out in recollections of *La Région Centrale*. As in these earlier films, Snow again has it both ways. The zoom in *Wavelength* tends to dehierarchize the film's events. Although the narrative is there to be read, the time, light events and the yellow chair have the same value as the human events. In ←——→ all events reiterate the basic panning gesture and are objectifications of it. Also, the mise-en-scène of *Wavelength* and the panning of ←——→ tend to equalize the contents and space of the frame. In *La Région Centrale* the constant movement of the camera dehierarchizes the contents of the frame. The relentless movement pulls away from a centre of attention, forcing the viewer to scan the frame. Thus despite the climaxes, and the beauty and variation of the landscape and the times of day, Snow effects within the fluid frame an equalizing or leveling, something akin to what Pollock did with abstraction in his overall drip paintings. Michael Fried's comments on Pollock seem appropriate and applicable to the effect of Snow's "frame movements."[9] "Pollock's all-over drip paintings refuse to bring one's attention to a focus anywhere. This is important. Because it was only the context of a style entirely homogeneous, all-over in nature and resistant to ultimate focus that the different elements in the painting—most important, line and colour—could be made... to function as wholly autonomous pictorial elements."[10]

Of course the Pollock reference is only an analogy. But Snow himself makes analogies to painting. In 1969 he wrote of his aspirations to execute a landscape film. "I want to make a gigantic landscape film equal in terms of film to the great landscape paintings of Cézanne, Poussin, Corot, Monet, Matisse and in Canada the Group of Seven...."[11] And after the shooting: "I wanted to make a film in which what the camera-eye did in the space would be completely appropriate to what it saw, but at the same time equal to it. Certain landscape paintings have achieved a unity of method and subject. Cézanne for instance produced an, to say the least, incredibly balanced relationship between what he did and what he (apparently) saw."[12] But any reference to Cézanne recalls the tension between the representational and the abstract. If Cézanne was involved with translating his vision onto canvas, Snow in his statement appropriately shifts the terms to what the camera does and what it sees. Snow's choice of landscape, the position of the camera and its point of view, and speeds of frame movements all combine to create a tension between the recorded landscape and the range of two-dimensional abstractions which are generated from it.

117

51. *La Région Centrale*
Photo: The National Gallery of Canada

Except for *New York Eye and Ear Control* which contrasts interior and exterior space, and ←——→ which begins with a short exterior shot, all other films discussed here were made in closed, controlled spaces. *La Région Centrale,* however, frames and surveys the wild landscape. The opening shot in section 1 gives the perceiver a clue as to how to approach the film. But it is no ordinary establishing or orientation shot. One might recall all those westerns which begin with a pan taken from a mountain top, slowly sweeping 150-180 degrees over valley, prairie or desert. The viewers feel they know the space almost well enough to inhabit it. But in Snow's film the camera slowly begins to record in detail the deep, rich red-brown colours of the rocky ground, circles gradually to include the shadow of the machine, moves up and out to the surroundings and finally to the sky, white and light blue and almost cloudless. The ground is flat and the sky appears flat too, flush to the frame when no colour or line sets up a figure-ground relationship. While the opening ground shot establishes clues for a visual theme, it does not orient the viewer to the landscape. The focus on flat ground or sky, and the speed and kinds of movements set up by Snow abstract the landscape and homogenize the overall field of the frame. The resulting scanning process prevents the viewer from locating a single focal point. Like the other films *La Région Centrale* works against deep space, even in this endlessly expansive, wild locale.

It is the preprogrammed camera that accomplishes all this. One becomes aware of the place of the machine with its ever-moving mounted camera from the occasional sight of its shadow. But is the viewer ever oriented to the landscape? One would expect the machine as centre point to create that orientation, but movement, framing and speed, while they serve to dissect space, do not achieve a synthesis of it. The camera "does" what it is scored to "see," but its sight is not bound by gravity. Just when the perceivers think they are acclimated in the space, for example when the camera moves at moderate speeds in short pans, the horizon turns, sky is at bottom, rocks at top so that sky looks like water and rocks like a sandy beach, or the image spins or spirals or the images pass by, one piece of land at one diagonal, a piece of sky at another diagonal.

There is no dissembling here. The camera creates the conjuring, and as in ←——→ it is a self-evident conjuring. *La Région Centrale* reveals the materials from which its abstractions come and by illusion—the shadow of the machine—the means of making the film. While the film has its levels of abstraction, it is always bound to the representational setting which it documents. Perhaps it could be said that we both know and don't know the space. That is, optically one has a sense of the topography of the

place but one is never located in it. Just as deep space is so frequently undermined, imaginary habitation of the space or a haptic sense of it is missing—gone as is gravity.

All these strategies seem to keep one outside as an observer of the camera's actions. They also make one aware, as Snow explains, of giving "the camera an equal role in the film to what is being photographed. . . . The camera is an instrument which has expressive possibilities in itself." And perhaps because of both factors—the role of the camera "equal" to what it photographs and the camera as a "separate expressive entity"[13]—one can still become involved and absorbed in the camera's spatial analyses as well as the drama it creates through its movements in the landscape.

If one becomes too involved, an X may appear at unpredictable moments, marking the divisions between sections, or the shadow of the machine may be glimpsed. Both the X and the shadow have self-reflexive purposes. The X brings one back to oneself, while the shadow reminds one of the making of the film. The X also acts formally to fix or stabilize the screen, and thus emphasizes the frame in another way. Moreover, it gives the perceiver a momentary respite from the otherwise continual frame movements. Both tactics seem to centre the viewer: while the X points to the self, the shadow of the machine also calls attention to the viewer's place and point of view. Speaking of the purpose of the X Snow remarks, "And in a way it's a title, a reminder of the central region—the whole thing is about being in the middle of this—the camera and the spectator."[14]

But then what is the central region? Is it a toponym or is it a metaphor for camera and spectator? Prior to the shooting of the film Snow wrote, "In complete opposition to what most films convey this film will not present only human drama but mechanical and natural drama as well." And after the shooting, "In *La Région Centrale* the frame emphasizes the cosmic continuity which is beautiful but tragic: it just goes on without us."[15]

In these few comments Snow equates camera and spectator, speaks of the presence of human drama and refers to the tragic quality of the location—which continues even in the absence of man. In effect isn't this anthropomorphism and anthropocentricism?

This is perhaps the major issue of *La Région Centrale*. One closely examines the making of the film and then considers the formal issues involving the machine, overall frame movement in the landscape, and sound. But this leads to the question of whether or not *La Région Centrale* is constructed anthropomorphically and anthropocentrically as Snow at times suggests.

Before finally deciding not to include the footage documenting the assembling of the machinery, Snow writes, "but after that we are gone and the remaining two and a half hours is entirely made by the machine (you?). There are no other people but you (the machinery?) and the extraordinary wilderness. Alone. Like a lot of other humans I feel horror at the thought of the humanizing of the entire planet. In this film I recorded the visit of some of our minds and bodies and machinery to a wild place but I didn't colonize it, enslave it. I hardly even borrowed it. Seeing really is believing."[16] Snow left out the "bodies." The landscape was explored by sight alone.[17]

In his essay "Nature, Humanism, Tragedy," Robbe-Grillet writes, "We know that the sense of touch constitutes, in everyday life, a much more *intimate* sensation than that of sight.... Optical description is, in effect, the kind which most readily establishes distances: the sense of sight, if it seeks to remain simply that, leaves things in their respective place."[18]

Robbe-Grillet's writings and ideas continue to be pertinent to the work of Snow. Robbe-Grillet rejects humanism of whatever ilk; he points out the ways in which man insists on establishing a single nature for himself and the world. Description of the world and its objects becomes corrupted by vocabulary which must see mountain, sun, valley in terms of man: "The mountain 'majestic,'...a 'pitiless' sun,...a village 'huddled' in the valley"(p.53). Such metaphor is the tool of humanism. It is used to expropriate all things to man so that the whole world participates in one and the same nature with him. Humanism employs analogy to dispose of distances and separations between man and the universe of things because man cannot bear these distances. Paradoxically, when man dwells upon and laments these distances, he analogizes again, destroying the distances he was aware of, projecting upon the world the sadness which only he as man feels. For his comfort and solace he tragedifies the world and in so doing ironically humanizes it.

In contradiction Robbe-Grillet writes, "Man looks at the world, and the world does not look back at him"(p.58). Hypothesizing about a character in a novel similar, not surprisingly, to a character in one of his own works, Robbe-Grillet describes the subject's attitude toward the world:

But now suppose the eyes of this man rest on things without indulgence, insistently: he sees them, but he refuses to appropriate them, he refuses to maintain any suspect understanding with them, any complicity; he asks nothing of them; toward them he feels neither agreement nor dissent of any kind. He can, perhaps, make them the prop of his passions, as of his sense of sight. But his sense of sight is content to take their measurements; and his passion similarly rests on their surface, without attempting to penetrate them since there is nothing inside, without feigning the least appeal since they would not answer (pp.52-53).

Robbe-Grillet attacks man's habit of filtering all things through himself. This hypothetical unity of man and universe points to a higher nature and thus to profundity, to a transcendence and inevitably to ineffability. All things in this one nature exist for man and have their meaning only in terms of man. Man is trapped into experiencing, observing, describing, using these things for himself, as they revolve around him. Things lose their separate existences and become a part of the "pre-established order" of humanism. Man's options and freedom become limited by this pananthropic view. In contrast, rejection of "nature, humanism, tragedy" is a freedom to see things as they are in their materiality, their uses, to describe them as form and substance, to see their surfaces and to "measure the distances—without futile regret, without hatred, without despair"(p.74). To assume this position, as Robbe-Grillet does, is to see rocks and boulders as rocks and boulders, sun as sun, moon as moon, sky as sky, a natural wilderness as a natural wilderness.

Description which does not use anthropomorphic metaphor is Robbe-Grillet's way of achieving this end in his writing, a way of "once again *facing* things"(p.71). On the other hand, Michael Snow seems to be ambivalent about *La Région Centrale:* some of his statements imply that his film is rooted within a humanist framework; others, that is stands outside of that traditional Renaissance-derived position.

But one must look to the work itself. In both subtle and blatant ways Snow abstracts his work through a variety of different devices. The constant frame movements force the viewer to scan the image, causing an overall homogeneity of frame space. Types and speeds of movement are also used to abstract the landscape being filmed. And although much of the time the landscape is recognizable, viewers never feel that they really know the space. *La Région Centrale,* one cannot forget, defies gravity. The film's three-hour length orchestrates the landscape. Through this dura-tion the camera analyzes the space—extending it and dividing it into ribbons of time. As in *One Second in Montreal* duration becomes another tool of abstraction.

One can interpret these formal devices as a means of assuming, respecting and finally preserving the distance between man and things. They of course are coupled with Snow's insistence on a wild locale untouched by man. They describe a topography— and are concerned with looking and seeing and not touching, inhabiting, colonizing, conquering. These formal means prevent

121

one from being lost or involved in the illusionistic spaces depicted. These spaces are formalized, subtly subverted, undermined and abstracted in degrees.

The X is another formal device. It acts as stabilizer or anchor for the frame and as antithesis to the frame movements. It also asserts the flatness of the screen. Like the machine's shadow, the X is a reflexive tool, recollecting the perceiver's awareness as the shadow recalls the process of film production. Yet do these devices suggest that this wild landscape and man share a common nature concerned with a transcendent humanistic enterprise, or do they preserve, and respect the distance between man and nature?

The hand of man is absent but the exploring camera expresses itself so that objective and subjective camera become one. The viewer is guided and manipulated by the camera which is unpredictable in its movements. Man's point of view is thus measured and distanced from the world by the camera.

Rather than centring man with the camera, thereby creating an anthropocentric metaphor, the X causes a closure, the flat surface blocking admission into the potentials of imaginary deep illusionistic screen space. It brings the perceivers back into themselves and away from the camera. The camera is not the surrogate for man.

There is then a triangulation which one can see from the formal and reflexive elements in the film. The perceiver is separate from the camera. The camera is centred and operates in trajectories of circles, arcs and lines in the expansive wilderness. It is centred to do what it is capable of doing then leaves, not conquering or taking over the land. Man-made, it sees how and what man cannot see unaided. Nature is the third term of the triangle. It is distanced from perceiver and camera. Man, conscious of himself and of the camera's place, does not centre himself in the landscape. The universe is not anthropocentric. Nature does not look back at man. It does not weep. *La Région Centrale* is not a pastoral elegy. Man is free to see in it the surfaces of nature, represented and transformed and transmogrified.

If one tragedifies nature in order to show its "otherness" from man, one ironically anthropomorphizes it. All things exterior to man assume their reality because of this surreptitious imposition of human traits upon them. One does not see the surface of a landscape, but only those curvatures which are like a human face—nature becomes one huge Mt. Rushmore. Many works of art have done this in the past and continue to do so. *La Région Centrale* does not identify man with nature. It uses nature in order to explore it, abstract it, reveal its beauty, its distance.

Chapter 8

"Hearing is Deceiving": Plane Sound and Light Talk in "Rameau's Nephew" by Diderot (Thanx to Dennis Young) by Wilma Schoen*

"Hey Abe, where's the voice coming from?"
"That piece of cheese spoke."
"It's that portrait of Winston Churchill on the wall."
"That iceberg in the snow scene on the calendar spoke."

Then sound and picture both literally slip out of frame, falling out of sight and sound in the office scene quoted from above, early on in *"Rameau's Nephew" by Diderot (Thanx to Dennis Young) by Wilma Schoen* by Michael Snow, as the participants in their comic maneuvers attempt to contain and reify the sound, while at the same time, filmmaker Snow introduces himself in the form of a pun.

In a short review of *"Rameau's Nephew"*. . . Bill Auchterlone speaks of containers as a major theme, not only in this work, but in Snow's other films as well.[1] Containers also suggest brackets and both become analogues for frames and framing in his work.

In sequence 18 of *"Rameau's Nephew"*. . . a woman stands framed at a window looking out at the rain. The airplane sequence begins with a voice saying "quote" and ends with "unquote", bracketing it off. In a long passage filled with an aura of mystery and intrigue and set in ornate eighteenth-century rooms, the spotlight is readjusted in the frame for each new shot, highlighting the sound and the posed elocutionist, thereby creating a tension or dynamic with light in the frame. As so often before in Snow's works, colour transparencies are used in a number of sequences. Sometimes they function to frame and to reframe the image as in the airplane, the loft and the hotel sequences. Framed numbers appear in several sections of the film, noting the occurrence of the homonyms: "four/for/fore/ 4." And in the tradition of Boccaccio, stories are framed: in the hotel sequence the old man with the violin tells his tale of Jesus and his wife to a cubist visual accompaniment, each of his syllables punctuated with an arbitrary cut to another object in the room, usually in a close-up shot. Tableaux, poses, events standing out in time, become analogues for the practice of framing.

*See Appendix D for a detailed description of the film by sequence.

52. *"Rameau's Nephew"*...
Sequence 3, Woman at piano
Photo: The National Gallery of Canada

53. *"Rameau's Nephew"*...
Sequence 7, Airplane
Photo: The National Gallery of Canada

In Renaissance tradition, the frame of a painting functioned as a metaphor for window, the perceiver looking out through the artwork to the world. As already discussed in terms of modernist art, container, frame, framing suggest the self-enclosed, a cutting off, the self-reflexive and the creation of an object commanding an existence of its own in the world. For minimal art which pronounced against metaphor and wished to free itself from the problems of illusionism, the issues are hypertrophied. Minimalism stands somewhere between modernism and post-modernism. It presents a commentary on the making of art objects through its use of industrial materials and its substitution of holistic and unitary structures in place of composition and fragmentation. The minimal work is abstract, but can also be seen as concrete in its clear and forceful immediacy and presence as an object.

In his photographic and certain of his film works, including *Wavelength* and ←——→ , Snow employs holistic and unitary structures (for instance, the zoom and the pan in these two films respectively as well as a single location in both) for art which is descriptive and literal. As already pointed out, while *Wavelength* reverberates the frame within the frame it also closes in on the photograph of ocean waves, punning on its title as it refers both to sound and colour waves. And ←——→ actualizes its title through the panning movement and its variations on back and forth, to and fro, hither and yon, in and out, falling back on itself and extending and contracting its space. While they can be read as objects, *Wavelength* and ←——→ also exist as processes unfolding in time, conveying the tension between the abstract and representational. In the way they manipulate dramatic and narrative forms they are implicit filmic deconstructions. They are also metaphors for how we come to know and understand. In this way each film moves beyond a formal reading as the frame echoes the tension of the work outside itself as an art object. While minimalism embraces the idea of the object as a whole, it eschews process and traces of making as counter to the finished and completed work. In contrast, object and process co-exist as important facets of much of Snow's work in film, photography and sound, as well as in his earlier paintings and sculptural pieces. Thus Snow sets himself off from minimalism in this and also another way: in minimal art illusionism and its forms are judged, if obliquely, through the exclusion of illusionistic references. But Snow includes the illusionistic in his films and photographs, making it one of the terms of a dialectic and a subject in his work.

Through these dialectical relationships of object and process, representational and abstract, an extremely important commen-

tary on illusionism is made at that meeting of modernism and post-modernism. The idea of a realism of process can be applied to the acts of making and perceiving in much of Snow's film and photographic work. The reflexive aspects of the realism of process of perception keep one analyzing the work and issues, taking apart the object, so that the illusion is not functioning in quite the same way: it is being examined and provides a critique of itself as it may also refer outside itself. *Wavelength* very well exemplifies those aspects of process.

The containment and framing in *"Rameau's Nephew"*... is quite different from that in *Authorization, Wavelength* or ←——————→. *"Rameau's Nephew"*... does not have the holistic structure of the others. It is built of many pieces—twenty-five in all. It is, to use Snow's word, "fragmented." He says, "It's a very, very broken up, fragmented kind of thing compared to the others. It's not as fragmented as many other films but in terms of the kinds of things that I've done, it's much more angular."[2]

While *"Rameau's Nephew"*... has much in common with Snow's other works stylistically, and while it is peppered with allusions to his other works, it is built and shaped differently. It is, in a sense, constructed from the outside in, rather than the reverse. *"Rameau's Nephew"*... is composed, orchestrated. Its parts are of unequal length and function. It doesn't frame itself as a complete object or process, concentrated and single in its direction. It strikes out, is uneven, unbalanced, points in many directions. But it builds on the ideas and implications of those past objects.

Unlike the descriptive, literal, sometimes punning titles of many of Snow's works which point to themselves, the title *"Rameau's Nephew" by Diderot (Thanx to Dennis Young) by Wilma Schoen* appears to function differently. Denis Diderot, philosopher, editor of the *Encyclopédie,* art critic, theorist of drama as well as author of several plays and other fiction, was a major intellectual figure of the eighteenth century in France. Dennis Young receives thanks because he gave Snow the copy of *Rameau's Nephew* by Diderot. Young was at that time a curator at the Art Gallery of Ontario in Toronto. Wilma Schoen is a pseudonym: *schoen* the German word for beautiful, Wilma Schoen an anagram for Michael Snow. Jean Philippe Rameau was a contemporary of Bach and Handel who contributed important theoretical writings on harmony, wrote harpsicord music, operas and opera ballets. He was for a time admired by the French intellectual circle which included Diderot, Rousseau and d'Alembert. And he did have a nephew, a would-be musician

126

and somewhat of a ne'er-do-well named Jean-François Rameau. This is the nephew of the title upon whom it is speculated that the "he" character in the book is based while the "myself," the first person in the dramatic dialogue, is the philosopher.

But after the title where does one continue with *"Rameau's Nephew"*. . .? Structure, use of language, representation? At the beginning of a short passage called "Passage," Snow writes: "Every beginning is arbitrary. I have noted in myself the emergence of the kind of attention I'm describing and called that a 'beginning.' I'll write more about that later." And at the very end of this brief text he says: "What's interesting is not codifying but experiencing and understanding the nature of passages from one state to another without acknowledging 'beginning' as having any more importance in the incident than 'importance' has in this sentence. Or than 'ending' in this."[3]

To change the function, to move from meaning to structure in words, in sentences, to shift categories thereby finding new meanings and structures. "Events take time. Events take place. One thing leads to another," Snow writes in "Passage." That statement most succinctly sums up the earlier *Wavelength*. Apart from describing Snow's more than four-hour film part by part, numerically, cross referencing allusions within it and through it to Snow's other works, critically it is extraordinarily difficult to begin discussing the film because of the fragmentation. "One thing leads to another" or one thing may refer back to a past sequence or forward to another, while still existing as a separate sequence in itself. And one's critical writing on the film begins to take on the tautological, oxymoronic qualities of the film.

One sequence in particular sums up many aspects of the film thus metaphorically suggesting the whole. This is the tabletop description, sequence 16, in which a woman in voice-over narrates the movement of objects on a large table top. The objects include stationery, stamps, glue, a roll of 16mm film, 35mm slides, videotape, rulers and brushes, pens and pencils, a typewriter, a Penguin paperback copy of Diderot's *Rameau's Nephew,* a folder marked "Rameau's Nephew," and a long rectangular black and white photograph in closeup of hands at a piano keyboard. The same hands, those of Snow himself, are at table's edge, poised at the right side of the screen frame as they move about the objects.

The woman's voice sounds variously like newscaster, sportscaster and forecaster as she sometimes leaps ahead of events, sometimes is behind, sometimes is in sync with the movements on the table top. In this way the verbal and visual double each other. At times objects are moved according to colour or shape. The

54. *"Rameau's Nephew"...*
Sequence 16, Tabletop
Photo: The National Gallery of Canada

array on the table looks chaotic. Objects are placed in a circle resembling a miniature wagon train; they are arranged and rearranged. At the end the objects are swept up and behind the typewriter. The same hands at the keyboard appear in a later sequence, the hotel suite (20), but as a moving rather than a still image, in colour, with sound but not that of the piano; and elsewhere in the same sequence keyboard music is heard, bringing to mind the absent still and movie images. The tabletop scene recalls *A Casing Shelved* in which Snow discusses various objects from his life as artist, many used in the course of his art-making activities. In *"Rameau's Nephew"*. . . the objects present all refer to the making of different kinds of discourses, potentially to making kinds of art—writing, video, painting, film, slides, drawing, etc. The narrated description of the moving of the objects rationalizes or orders the observed actions. The scene itself becomes quite comic. The title on the paperback cover is nearly impossible to read unless one has seen it previously, although with the *Rameau's Nephew* folder present one might guess that the book is not an arbitrary choice. Occurring two-thirds through the film this sequence uses verbal description as a form of doubling and toys with fragmentation and disorder. And there is the two-fold reference to the film itself and to the Diderot text, as if to remind one of the importance of the title, and of the importance of Diderot's text to the film.

The Diderot text is indeed relevant. Concerning the dramatic dialogue between the philosopher identified in the text as "myself" and the artist (Rameau's nephew) referred to as "he," a critical debate has been waged about which, if either, is the persona for Diderot. To identify "myself" with Diderot is to jump to facile conclusions; to associate the "he" with Diderot leaves too many gaps. The philosopher stands on the side of reason; the ne'er-do-well musician-nephew on that of passion. They represent opposite tendencies in their discourse and deportment.

Myself—Philosopher	*He-Artist*
Reason	Passion and feeling
Mind	Body
Logical and analytical thinking	Synthetic function of the imagination, artistic expression
Logic	Paralogic and sophisms
Language	Gesture

The most interesting critical speculation is that the dialogue represents a synthesis of Diderot's two roles in the Enlightenment: as co-editor of the *Encyclopédie,* as art and drama critic and as philosopher on the one hand, and as dramatist and author of fictional texts on the other. This interpretation is reinforced by Diderot's use of *dédoublement* in his theories and fiction, that is, the dialectic he thought so essential between reason and emotion, analysis and synthesis, critical distance and identification.[4]

In Diderot's *Rameau's Nephew* there is the dialogue with the self reflected in the work, the control and logic of the philosopher, a bit plodding in his thinking and in his language, and the excesses and gestures of the artist always checking the philosopher. The dialogue ends with these delightfully amusing passages: The artist has just spoken of his deceased wife. ("At which he began to sob and choke as he said: 'No, no, I never shall get over it. Ever since, I've taken minor orders and wear a skull-cap.' ")

Myself: From grief?

He: If you like. But really in order to carry my soup plate upon my head. . . .

He: Farewell, Master Philosopher, isn't it true that I am ever the same?

Myself: Alas! Yes, unfortunately.

He: Here's hoping this ill fortune lasts me another forty years. He laughs best who laughs last.[5]

Running through Snow's *"Rameau's Nephew"*. . . is a philosophical discussion about reality, appearance, illusion, representation, verisimilitude, which is undercut by humour in the form of sophisms, paralogisms, puns, repetition, variation, excess. Snow plays with reason and logic in his films; the imaginative object is the synthesis of various kinds of meaning and expression, the result of the play with reason and logic.

Snow scripted all of *"Rameau's Nephew"*. . . . He also used professional actors and actresses in two sequences—the four participants in the tea party (12) and four of the performers in the hotel suite (20).

Snow refers to the film as a "talking picture." It is very much about kinds of sound and kinds of sound-visual relationships. The recorded sound is representational and abstract involving music, speech, animal calls, other outdoor as well as machine noises. Sync and non-sync sound are used. And there is a wide range of variation in the uses of sync sound: playing sync material backwards, as in 12; recording undecipherable speech patterns as in sequence 9 (Burton), cataloguing sounds made through breath and speech exercises as in 1 (Snow whistling) and 15 (the embassy). It also records pissing and sink sounds.

How does one read the sound? The film is "For English Speaking Audiences Only," according to the subtitle. Yet following Snow's whistling, the rest of the preface is given in other languages, save for the Beatles who are quickly tuned out. The act of reading is very much a part of the film in its references to book structure. In occidental reading patterns one's eyes move left to right and top to bottom on the page; mere traditional reading habits are eschewed by the credits which pass upward on a roller on the screen, superimposed over freight trains passing right to left. In book fashion a dedication and sources are given: "Dedicated to Alexander Graham Bell" and "Based on the *Decameron* by Boccaccio and the *Bhagavad Gita*." There are distinct sequences of varying lengths similar to chapters or to essays in a collection. The counting of the homonyms "four/4/fore/for" act as footnotes. They are tallied at the end in sequence 21 in academic style by P. Adams Sitney, followed by an erratum (24) and an addendum (25). And the Mental Profumo L'Alito tin appears after the credits as 5 and then as 22, sandwiched between Sitney's counting and Snow's curtain call and signature in 23. The Mental Profumo L'Alito container brackets off the main body of the text.

In comments on the film dated November 1974 Snow stated: "Thus its 'dramatic' development derives not only from a representation of what may involve us generally in life but from considerations of the nature of recorded speech in relation to moving light images of people. Thus it can become an event *in life*, not just a report of it." (Italics mine.) And in a letter to Jonas Mekas printed in his "Movie Journal" in the *Village Voice,* February 3, 1975, he writes: "My films are intended to be unique experiences, actual despite their being representational, but also because they're representational. That's what they work with. An aspect of them is that they provoke meanings. Especially *'Rameau's* etc.' which far more than any of my other films is the other half of a dialogue."[6]

Both quotations return one to Diderot. For "the event" and the "unique experience" read also object; add to this the idea of "meaning" along with "dialogue." The event is set off, framed as object yet is a sign containing meaning—this is something of the task with which Diderot was concerned,[7] something of the input into modernism for which Diderot is heralded and credited today. And the object-meaning relationship is itself a dialogue. But another dialogue concerns itself with the mind-body split familiar from Diderot's dramatic dialogue in *Rameau's Nephew*. The mysterious Mental Profumo L'Alito box appears in the only wholly silent sequences, 5 and 22 (the silent chromatic

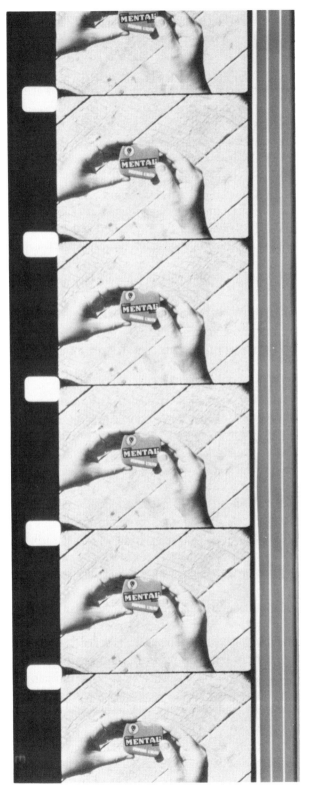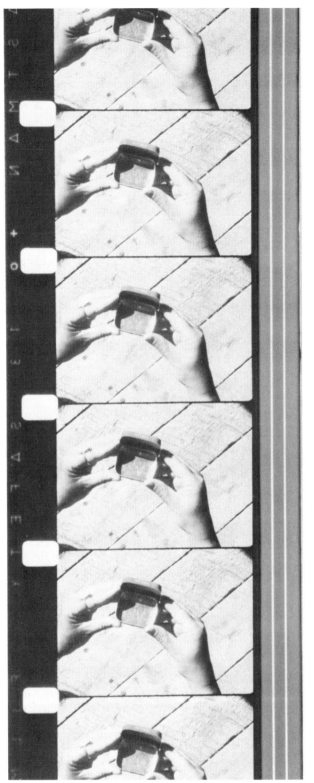

flicker and non-flicker anacruses not considered here), which are set aside as brackets, quotation marks. For an English-speaking audience they offer a double play, a dialogue and a pun suggesting the awkwardly literal sense of a mental refreshment for the spirit or mind and then its real meaning translated as mentholated mints for the breath; in fact the film is a dialogue about ideas and recorded speech. And in his curtain call (23), before the erratum, Snow displays "cymbal," "orange" and yellow followed by a snow-covered car. These serve as homonyns and puns but also literally and descriptively return the film to its object status; here it is what it is *but* also means. "Seeing is believing." "Hearing is deceiving" is thrown about in 20, the hotel sequence, and something of the point of the puns, homonyms, and broad and literalizing humour is made clear.

As pointed out earlier Snow has consistently worked with representational or referential imagery in his films and yet had it both ways, that is, moving back and forth between the abstract and the representational. And here he shifts into sound relationships—abstract and representational, sound-visual relationships—abstract and representational, and, as he puts it, with recorded speech and "scales of 'intelligibility.'"[8]

What are the criteria for intelligibility of sound, of speech? Are the criteria only audial or also visual? The question again recalls Diderot in the dialogue between language and gesture and the importance of the two.

The bus, tea party and Indian village mock-up appear in a row as sequences 11, 12 and 13. While they are quite separate one can see important relationships among them. In the bus sequence, as the voice-over with the lisp lectures about systems of greater and greater verisimilitude and machine reproduction similar to human reproduction so that illusion and reality will be indistinguishable, pockmarks show up increasingly on the image with occasional end roll dots; the time for the lecturer's speculations seems very far away. It appears even farther away in the tea party sequence. The illusionistic image is confounded by the speech which is recited backwards while the film is printed tail to head. It is abstracted, but one can make out words backwards and frontwards—"god"/"dog," "tish"/"shit," "amora"/"aroma," "tac"/"cat," and on the return only: "Without recourse to metaphor or simile could you describe the scent? Is this the fart of vision?" which one might pick out if not the first time then on subsequent screenings of the film. One cannot ignore allusion to Brakhage's *Art of Vision* nor to his aesthetic shaped by sight with a general distaste for sound, sound used only three times in his films in the past dozen years. The "fart of vision" in this section is

133

57. *"Rameau's Nephew"*. . .
Sequence 12, Tea party
Photo: Michael Snow

not quite as oxymoronic as one might at first think. It is the gestures, for want of deciphering the sound, which inform one about the meaning of the tableau: the use of the spray can, sniffing, the proper poses of the participants and their gentility being disrupted. One can hear a great deal in the replay of the second half of the sequence tail to head as the words and sentences are given in their proper order—though one must listen carefully several times to follow. But still it reminds one of Diderot's comment that he liked to watch a very familiar theatre piece with his hands over his ears as a way of testing the actors' effective use of gestures for conveying meaning, and also his parallel "comparison between the beholder of a painting and a deaf person watching mutes converse on subjects known to him."[9] Here gesture aids language and carries the general meaning of the tableau, a form of *dédoublement,* through a dialogue between the body and the mind.[10] Through the first half, spoken backwards, one has only the gestures to go on; with the inversion, words are intelligible. The symmetry reveals the process involved in the work, the second half making clear how

134

58. *"Rameau's Nephew"*. . .
Sequence 8, Sink
Photo: The National Gallery of Canada

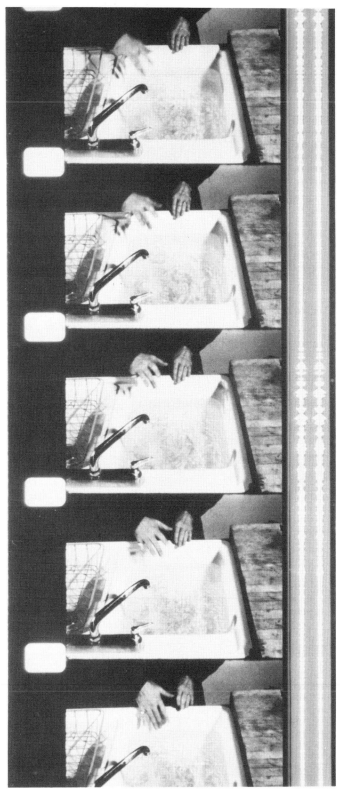

the work was made. But the symmetry, beginning at the camera eye and returning and ending there, also encloses the work formally. Stylistically one thinks of the two-screen work, *Two Sides to Every Story,* and also the photographic book, *Cover to Cover.* And sound becomes curiously hypostasized in so far as it also serves to enclose the sequence as object or tableau.

But as one moves to sequence 13, the Indian village mock-up, sound and visual material stand even further away from the verisimilitude of which the lisping lecturer in voice-over on the bus speaks, as voices, noises, animal calls and colours of clothing of the participants are more and more abstracted. "This is really artificial. There is nothing natural about it," says a voice at the onset. ". . . it's the abstraction and it shows that the colour of that yellow shirt is yellow light. What's standing for the yellow shirt is yellow light," Snow commented.[11] Volume and pitch are adjusted and voices become music or noise, for abstraction of sound and visuals are analogous; they are not as clearly revealed as is the sound procedure in sequence 12, although one is aware of the continual breakdown of the representational sounds and images. They both move toward creation of the object and immediacy.

In the sink sequence (8), sync sound is sink sound which is a pun and a rebus as well. It is what it is. Music is made. In the following sequence, Dennis Burton reads in sync an almost totally undecipherable text as various colours from a video process flicker as a form of interference on certain consonant sounds and at certain volumes. Near the end Snow's off-screen voice interjects: "Would you say that reality has the same limitations as our methods of observation?" and Burton answers in the affirmative, repeating Snow's words resyllabified to reveal the procedure. The words are in order, but emphasis and accent have been changed, beginnings of words added to ends, new divisions made. When Burton finishes, Snow barks like a dog and Burton responds with what one hears as "Whorf?" a pun alluding to Benjamin Lee Whorf, an amusing twist to the positivist, empirical question posed by Snow and affirmed by Burton, as one is conveniently enough reminded of Whorf's most appropriate title, *Language, Thought and Reality.* On reading Burton's text one discovers that it is in fact tautological, stating that words represent external events which are in turn symbolized by words, and so on.

Realism of process and literal word plays are incorporated into and then undercut in sequence 10, the loft. The projection of the short film three times within the sequence assists in sorting out the rather confused layers of repetitions and additions of voices, music and noise. Acts of seeing objects and hearing voices and music are questioned. Scripts are read. Layers of sounds accumulate but the build-up is not dramatic. It becomes an irritant most difficult to listen to. The frame is very carefully composed. The camera is stationary, filming in medium-long shot from a frontal position. People hover on the sides of the screen frame, sometimes cut off, or a table is partially out of frame. A green acetate transparency is moved around the room—on the back wall, on the table, in hand, in front of the lens when a short film is projected through it, so that sometimes it is very consciously used to frame or reframe the image.

The projections of the film appear distinctly different each time, as an anacrusis preceding this sequence, and three times as film-within-the- film: from the rear wall; from the camera's point of view toward the rear wall through the green filter; and from right to left side, as they contain the tableau and sequence. The projections subtly build the sequence into a virtual three-dimensional or sculptural shape. And in another way, the taped repetitions of speech, music and other sounds take the sequence out of time, aurally contributing to the object-like sense. The visual-aural complex in this sequence becomes over-all sculptural, while at the same time hearing and listening are the issues, as are seeing and looking at, while instruments of discourse, communication and reproduction are very much visible—tape recorder, record player, speakers, telephone, projector, typewriter.

The way the object is shaped in the tea party sequence stands out from the loft as also from the plane sequence (7). "I may be putting words into your mouth, but," says the voice of Snow offscreen as the exterior of an airplane appears and a woman says, "quote" and the image cuts to the interior for plane sound and plain speech. Commonplaces, clichés, puns abound about food, drink, vacations, time as then, now, again, before, plays on planes of reality, quality and style, airplanes, plainsong, explaining, plain as simple, with plays on homonyms such as here/hear, on tense and person as a word is worked with very simply and literally. For instance:

Harry: Alf, I don't understand what you mean, but I need to be seen.

Debbie: You are.

Natalie: Alf, I don't understand what you meant.

Alf: Some creature would have to come from somewhere else to give us an objective opinion.

Harry: Don't you see, Natalie? (hand-wave motion)

Natalie: I see Debbie, she said. I see Alf.

137

Alf: So do I but that's not the point. (points anywhere)

Debbie: Well I'm Debbie and I don't see *her* very well. So what's the point?

Alf: Nobody knows and they can think what they can think.

Natalie: Some people claim to know.

Debbie: Don't you agree, Alf?

Alf: I dunno.

Natalie: Why not?

Alf: I've changed my mind. (points at head)

Debbie: Into what?

Alf: It doesn't know.

Natalie: Why don't you let it speak for itself?

Harry: My mind senses an added complexity to what I think you meant, Alf. If there was a commentator-observer from elsewhere we'd both need an interpreter as well.

Alf: Dolphin.

Debbie: I . . .

Natalie: But . . .

Debbie: What's the meaning of it all?

Natalie: I don't know what to say.

Debbie: It's beyond me.

Natalie: What were you going to say?

Near the end comments are made. Debbie: "This will soon be over." Alf: "It's always nearly over." Harry: "That's over." And later Alf: "Go ahead. It's always just beginning." Paradoxically, both comments about beginning and ending are descriptive of the sequence structure. Camera movement and cutting on phrases and sentences in tilts, pans, diagonals, zooms from person to person or to objects give the sequence an appearance of always either beginning or ending. Later Snow is heard on the sound track assigning lines to be spoken by each person, one by one, as he literally puts words into the participants' mouths. Lines are repeated by different speakers. "Unquote," says a woman's voice. "Kind of leaves you up in the air, doesn't it?" says Harry, one of the performers, at the end in voice-over. In terms of Snow's use of the camera, one thinks of *La Région Centrale, Standard Time* and ←——→. A Doppler-like effect is used, with distortions of pitch and volume, sometimes making voices at either extreme of volume unintelligible; one is reminded here of the distortions in the "focus" and the Indian village mock-up sequences. While in the loft sequence the projections sculpt and contain the scene and the repetitions of sound layers all enforce the object quality, here the clichés, banalities, one-dimensionality, combined with the repetitions have a flattening effect.

In his text Snow reveals the ventriloquist role he has stylized for himself. "I may be putting words into your mouth, but," "quote" and "unquote." In a somewhat different vein, one is reminded again of Diderot. Diderot had conceived of the actor as puppet, playing within the scene rather than declaiming out at the audience. The actor was separate from his audience. While Diderot proposed a form of realism for a bourgeois theatre, he saw acting as stylized gestures and speech, perfected, honed down to the meaning of the action. His theory of acting worked hand in hand with the play as composed of self-enclosed scenes or tableaux.[12] In his way Snow exaggerates the idea of actor or puppet here and in other sequences as well.

For instance, in the two English comedians sequence (19), a voice or audience laughter and applause dictates the shots used. The same trio, two men and a woman, appear in each of the three shots. One man is sitting puppet-like on the other's lap. The shots change from one to another on one or the other voice, or on audience laughter and applause. The images are also coded to primary colours: one shot is side lit in blue, another side lit in red, while the third, on audience laughter and applause, is front lit in white light so that the woman's yellow sweater stands out. The accent of the comedians is difficult for many English people to understand let alone Americans and Canadians. Ironically, by listening long and attentively enough one can hear one of the comedians saying to the other at the end, "You can't just look religious. You must think religious too." In this way, they reintroduce the question of appearance, reality and perception so well articulated in Snow's question and Burton's affirmative response.

Appearance seems to confound reality in more than one sequence of "Rameau's Nephew".... The embassy sequence (15) has an aura of mystery about it. The setting and the participants are two of its contributing ingredients, as another version of sound and gestural gaming continues. The eighteenth-century drawing rooms used here were formerly part of the Soviet Embassy in New York, presently the Center for Inter-American Relations where Snow had had a large exhibition in 1972. Artist Nam June Paik, called Tom in the script, film critic Annette Michelson referred to as Gloria, and filmmakers Bob Cowan as Peter and Helene Kaplan as Vivian are the principles. Another woman, Yoko Orimoto, known in the script as Alexia,

59. *"Rameau's Nephew"*...
Sequence 19, English comedians
Photo: The National Gallery of Canada

60. *"Rameau's Nephew"*. . .
Sequence 15, Embassy
Photo: Michael Snow

is more passive, hovering around the edges and back of the frame most of the time. At the end Gloria announces to all, "I'm worried that the people next door may have a wine glass up against the wall and be listening to us."

Peter: Does that work?

Tom: I don't understand.

Gloria: I'll show you what I mean. (She holds up a glass.) Here (to Alexia), Alexia. You try it. Just put the big part of the wine glass up against the wall and your ear to the other and listen. (Alexia does so, returns and sits down).

Gloria: Did you hear anything?

And the sequence ends as mysteriously as it began. What did Alexia hear? What would the person on the other side of the wall have heard? What was Gloria worried about? Elegant drawing rooms; a strange cast. Is there a message to be decoded? One awaits the solution to the mystery but it never comes.

The catalogue of sounds continues in this sequence: burping, yawning, snoring, sneezing, etc., as the elocutionists are dramatically spotlighted gesticulating each utterance. Chickens cackling,

141

music from a "huge orchestra" and Bob Dylan's "A Hard Rain's A-Gonna Fall" come from a cassette tape recorder passed around and flung from a table. The recorder is also highlighted. Homonyms of *for* are counted again. The constant light focus on the sound source solves none of the mystery.

The participants assume stage-like positions. While grouped together or performing acts together they appear isolated and unrelated. Each of the performers stands out from the other in appearance and in style. Nam June Paik plays a straight comic role next to Annette Michelson as the academic, pedantic in her tone of voice, lecturing at one time on "interesting subjects," and at another giving the meanings of the word *chair,* including "a learned position like our professorial 'chair.'" Alexia might as well be called Aphasia for she says not one more word throughout, though it may be her voice uttering a few lines in Japanese early in the sequence while she is hidden from camera view. She is very much the object. But so are the more active four in the ways that they are manipulated by light, by one another, and the way they themselves manipulate speech and other sound exercises. At one point Cowan is shaken and manipulated by Paik, Kaplan and Michelson as he is made to appear like a puppet, and later he becomes ventriloquist for Michelson who mouths his words to "O Canada." The light and sound men, visible in each shot, shift positions on each new shot, thereby recomposing each and controlling the frame. Camera positions change as well. It is as if the microphone and small hand spotlight were controlling the participants.[13] The images are very carefully framed with tensions set up in one or another corner of the screen frame, a scene centred, then thrown slightly off balance on the next shot, all based around the sound source being keyed by the light man.

"Did you hear anything?" may in fact be addressed to the audience. The setting and the participants offer the ingredients of an intrigue—"For English Speaking Audiences Only." The sounds are illuminated, figuratively speaking, but are never decoded. Light only emphasizes the sounds; they are what they are but still remain mysterious. One is thwarted in any attempt to organize the sequence and sounds in order to create a causality; yet the sequence has its own internal dynamic. It is a series of tableaux of drawing-room games which we as audience observe. The line "This is really artificial. There is nothing natural about it" refers as much to this as to the Indian village mock-up sequence in which it is uttered.

Snow sums up his question "Would you say that reality has the same limitations as our methods of observation?" in the hotel suite sequence (20), the last one in the body of the text before P.

142

Adams Sitney tallies *four* homonyms. It is the least self-enclosed sequence, as it restates questions already posed and refers to past sections. Trumpet music replaces a line of dialogue as a participant says, "I didn't know you spoke trumpet." One recalls Snow on trumpet in the airplane sequence (7) as well as Snow the actual trumpeter. References are made to "that article" about illusionism and "that article" about "our inventing new species," as the viewer thinks of the text read on the bus (11). Names of birds are recited, recalling the bird whistles in 1 and bird calls in sequence 13. On an optical flip one of the participants says, "There's another side to every story," suggesting the tea party sequence (12) as well as Snow's earlier *Two Sides to Every Story* and his book *Cover to Cover*. Snow's hands at the keyboard recall the photograph in the table top description (16), and like the trumpet remind one that Snow is active as a musician.

"I may be putting words into your mouth, but" from sequence 7 is reworked here in another form. Two women repeat lines given through earphones, Sarah quoting Mao from "Where Do Correct Ideas Come From?" and Sarah and Eva quoting a dialogue from Jane Austen's *Pride and Prejudice*. And the comical attempt in the office sequence (6) to reify sound returns quite literally with a bang: earphones are placed on the green table as Leon says, "If that table could talk," and smashing is heard, apparently coming from the earphones. "It only remembers the pain," says Sarah. "Perhaps the pleasure was all ours," remarks Leon.

Punning continues very much in the style of the plane sequence. For instance, there is a play on the name Aphasia (as loss of power to use words) and on the device of the fade in and fade out:

FADE IN

Jacques: Aphasia, do you think it's nearly always over?

FADE OUT

Aphasia: I don't know . . . couldn't say.

FADE IN

Eva: No, it's me that couldn't say.

FADE OUT

Aphasia: Alright, I don't know. . . . I can't say.

FADE IN

Eva: Say it isn't so. (There are no fades here)

Aphasia: (Shouts) It's not!

143

Sounds and images are exchanged and displaced. These become ways of fabricating relationships within and across the sequence. The table smashing is heard while the earphones are on the table, yet only dialogue produced in a previous scene in this sequence is heard as Ray actually smashes the table. Through subtle displacements relationships occur through music. A Duke Ellington composition called "Daydream" is played about one-quarter of the way through the sequence. At one point its melody is picked up and played on a violin; at another point chords from it are strummed on a guitar. The same music is performed on the piano over the image of Sarah in bed silently mouthing the names of colours which are simultaneously projected over her image in the form of translucent filters. Later her voice is heard naming these colours, accompanying an intercourse scene in close-up, while at another point a woman's voice, apparently in the course of orgasm, is combined with the image of Snow's hands playing the piano. Earlier the word *Armageddon* replaces a note on a guitar and at another point a guitar substitutes for *Armageddon*, like the trumpet replacement for a sentence.

"This film looks like it was hewn with an axe," the old Jacques says early on. "Edited with an axe is the way we in the movies would put it," says Leon. Snow plays with the image very literally. When the image is optically flipped, those who were in the image and are now fictively displaced on the other side talk about what it is like to be on the other side. People and objects appear and disappear through superimposition. The old Jacques, violinist and storyteller, is metamorphosed through superimposition into the young Jacques, the rake who looks the entrepreneur, the artiste-prestidigitator and is, in a word, a ham.

Snow outrageously takes the philosophical arguments about appearance and reality and truth to comically absurd lengths through literal demonstrations on film. The "real" and "ideal" tables of philosophy are replaced by the image of the table on film in its states, that is, as first generation representational image, and as twice removed in superimposition. For instance, we as audience see it twice removed as superimposition, while on screen in the fiction some see it in a dialogue trying to prove its existence to others on screen who don't. Table variously becomes a "vege-table," a "multiplication table," a "veri-table." But is there and is it a "veri-table"? Here the table humorously becomes a working truth put to question. The table becomes the "problematic." Is there a "veri-table"? Extrapolating the sophisms of this sequence into absurdities, that is only so if "eating is believing" and that table was used, thus the truth is in the table. Throughout the sequence "seeing is believing" is questioned and "hearing is deceiving" is established as sounds are mismatched.

The punning carries on throughout the sequence with discussions about and demonstrations using tables and beds. At one point Jacques says, "I suppose we all believe that there's a bed there (points) and that it actually exists."

Eva: Of course, I slept there last night and had wonderful dreams. (Jacques walks to where the bed is supposed to be and lies down as if the bed were there, so that his feet will stick out when the bed is put back. The others gape. In superimposition the bed is then put back in place over Jacques.)

FADE IN

Eva (off screen): Well that proved that his was a dream and that that's a comfortable bed.

Aphasia: Who said that?

Jacques (getting up): Well we usually use a table to demonstrate reality.

Eva: That's because a table is more real than a bed at dinner time.

Jacques: What time is it?

Sarah: Time for bed.

FADE OUT

Near the end of the sequence Ray asks: "Is this film art?" And Eva responds: "No this is not art. It was once, but now nature is art." Is this a colloquialization of Pope's "All Nature is but Art unknown to thee?" Or is it a wry response to the "article" read in voice-over in the bus sequence which can easily be seen as a parody of Bazinian thinking about how film and photography are set apart from the other arts through automatism, that is, the freedom from interference of man's hand in the registration of the picture-taking process. But the article goes much beyond Bazin: the image is not only a transference but a form of phylogenesis of mechanical life through an anthropomorphic symbiosis of the technological. It is a new totality concept, an ironic return to an epic realism through the machine in the technological age. Toward the end of the sequence Ray is watching TV and Leon says: "Did you read that article about illusionism? It said that things like this would get more and more realistic until you wouldn't be able to tell the difference between me and a movie of me."

But Snow's procedures throughout the film have been very much in an opposite direction, a critique of realism and verisimilitude and a very sophisticated response to the problems of

145

illusionism. Is "seeing believing?" "Hearing is deceiving" stresses the fact that sound has often been neglected or taken for granted in film. After all, Bazin was talking about "the myth of total realism," speaking of the historically accidental focus on the image rather than on sound. And if one recalls that Edison invented his kinetoscope as a visual accompaniment for his phonograph, one has to consider the components of realism. Film illusionism has an audial and a visual component. Throughout the film Snow has toyed with synchronous and asynchronous sound, often in humorous forms such as puns and comic clichés. He has made, in a sense, a comic book. And through the sound, Snow the author is very much there behind the work as ventriloquist controlling the whole, cover to cover.

Snow has built on the problems and issues presented in his work of the 1960s. The holistic and unitary structuring of *Wavelength* and ←———→ with their single and concentrated preoccupations is replaced here in *"Rameau's Nephew" by Diderot (Thanx to Dennis Young) by Wilma Schoen* with brackets—the Mental Profumo L'Alito tin, quotes and containers within containers. The parts are uneven in weight, they stick out and refer to one another. It becomes a research film fully equipped with pedagogical apparati—footnotes, erratum, addendum—while at the same time it pokes fun at the pedantic uses of such devices.

The appearance of Diderot's name and his title in Snow's title is commonly interpreted to indicate that the film is encyclopedic in its uses of sound. Perhaps more interesting is the film's multiple uses of structuring, of ordering section by section, and its implicit questioning of ways of ordering and structuring. But encyclopedia also implies information and knowledge as does the book form which Snow chose. And the keys to that knowledge are the homonyns and puns playing on connotation and denotation, understanding and misunderstanding, sign and symbol, the visual and the aural, logic-order and humour-sophism in the exchange which takes place between language and gesture and mind and body in Wilma Schoen's Diderotian dialogue by Michael Snow.

Conclusion

61. *Flight Stop*. This very recent architectural sculpture is constructed of photographs glued to fiberglass forms. It is installed in Eaton Centre, Toronto.
Photo: Michael Solomon

It has been four years since the completion of Michael Snow's last film, *Breakfast*, and six since his last major film, "Rameau's Nephew"... His time has been taken up with music and photographic works. He expects to begin a new film within a matter of months. Nevertheless, Snow's four principal films dating from 1966 through 1974 have made him one of the major figures of the film avant-garde in North America, together with Maya Deren, Jonas Mekas, Stan Brakhage and Andy Warhol.

Snow's *Wavelength* has already become a classic, not only of the avant-garde cinema but also of cinema history in general. But dealing with *Wavelength* and with Snow's other films has not been easy for most critics. Ghettoizing his works within the film avant-garde or looking at them askance from the perspective of normative cinema does them an injustice and allows no space for the expansive issues they raise. It is too easy to ghettoize the avant-garde. Too often a closed dialogue takes place within this other cinema in which figures are heroized, works exalted, claims bent out of historical context and proportion. Taking such a defensive posture finally does more critical and historical damage than good and is a trap I have worked purposely to avoid in this book.

Snow works in many media and because of this figures within the larger art world. There has always been a dialogue of shared issues among his works in different media—between painting and film, film and photography, photography and painting, etc. Rejecting as inadequate the conventional critical options within film for treating Snow's works, I drew the long composite picture of two directions of formalist thinking in the visual arts and literature. Snow could then be located within the more expansive "continental" expression of formalism as articulated by Malevich, Shklovsky, Léger, Robbe-Grillet (and including Peckham, though American), rather than the restrictive Anglo-American one represented by Bell, Fry, the New Critics and Greenberg. Deformation, discontinuity, defamiliarization, the active role of the perceiver, and the importance and meaning of new forms are critical ideas running through this thinking which have their analogues in Snow's film and photographic works.

These general ideas work very well with specific issues in his work such as framing, the object, process, the literal and the descriptive, distancing, uses of autobiography and the anti-romantic. In my analysis I tried to apply the force and meaning of

147

those general ideas to these specific issues in the films and photographic pieces.

Snow's work is timely. It rides on the edge of modernism into the post-modern period. *"Rameau's Nephew"*. . . in particular explodes in its fragments to address various questions about reading and hearing even while it is still carefully composed formally. The figure of Diderot points explicitly to the modernist debate at the same time suggesting the tug-of-war between modernism and post-modernism. Snow's art at its best, like the nephew and philosopher in Diderot's *Rameau's Nephew*, brings together the physical, sensuous and perceptual, as represented by the body, with the intellectual. Snow's is an intellectual art with strong perceptual appeals. In its fullness it has both.

I hope that through this analysis Snow will be seen a little more clearly by those who couldn't see him at all before. And for those who have always seen Snow with some clarity and admiration, I hope that *Snow Seen* will enhance their understanding and pleasure in seeing old and new Snows.

Notes

See Bibliography for complete bibliographical details of sources cited here.

Chapter 1

1. Alain Robbe-Grillet, *For a New Novel*, p. 43.

2. *Transparent cinema* is used throughout the text to mean a cinema shaped in such a way as to reduce as much as possible the distance between it and the perceiver, as well as all formal means which would enhance such distance. It is realistic cinema of the highest possible degree of illusionism and involvement. Metaphorically the screen becomes a thin clear veil separating the perceiver from the world on the other side.

3. Michael Snow, *Michael Snow/A Survey*, p. 84.

4. *A to Z* (1956). 16mm. 4 min. blue and white, silent. Snow's one-line comment on the film in *Film-Makers' Cooperative Catalogue No. 5*, p. 298, reads: "A cross-hatched animated fantasy about nocturnal furniture love. Two chairs fuck." It is a kinetic version of Snow's earlier pen and ink series entitled *Metamorphosing Furniture*. The alphabet is the a priori structure, anticipating in rudimentary form the exploratory a priori forms Snow would begin to use a few years later.

5. Snow, *Michael Snow/A Survey*, p. 12.

6. Ibid., p. 15.

7. See Appendix A for complete text.

8. This unfinished film was financed by Ben Parks who, according to Snow, still has the several hours of footage.

9. *Short Shave* (1965). 16mm. 4 min. b&w, sound. In *Film-Makers' Cooperative Catalogue No. 5*, p. 299, Snow comments, "Vanity. Had a beard. Appearance (looks). Looking. Disappearance act. Hand-made fades and zooms but camera made shave. Camerazor. Handsome. Tired. Walking Woman. My worst film."

10. Brydon Smith, ed., *Michael Snow/Canada*, p. 19.

Chapter 2

1. Gene Youngblood, *Expanded Cinema*, p. 126.

2. See Peter Wollen, "Cinema and Semiology: Some Points of Contact," in *Movies and Methods*, ed. Bill Nichols, pp. 481-92.

3. André Bazin, *What is Cinema?* vol. 1, pp. 17-22.

4. Peter Wollen, *Signs and Meaning in the Cinema*, p. 122. Wollen refers to C.S. Pierce's definition of index as a sign "by virtue of an existential bond between itself and its object."

5. Bazin, p. 13.

6. Ibid., p. 15.

7. Siegfried Kracauer, *Theory of Film*, p. x.

8. Ibid., p. ix.

9. It should be noted that often when Bazin and Kracauer, especially Kracauer, speak of documentary, realism, naturalism and neorealism, they are speaking

of a transparent cinema whose characteristics are related to those of classical Hollywood realism, to the popular commercial entertainment cinema with which Panofsky and Cavell are concerned. See n. 15 below.

10. Kracauer, pp. 20-28.

11. Erwin Panofsky, "Style and Medium in the Motion Pictures," pp. 31-32.

12. Ibid., p. 30.

13. Stanley Cavell, *The World Viewed.*

14. See, for example, Greenberg's *Art and Culture,* especially "Avant-Garde and Kitsch," pp. 3-21; "Modernist Painting," *Arts Yearbook,* pp. 103-08; and "After Abstract Expressionism," *Art International,* pp. 24-32.

15. It is essential to note the difference between the traditional use of the term *realism* by Bazin and Kracauer and its radically different use by artists, critics and historians in twentieth-century movements such as cubism, suprematism, constructivism, neo-plasticism, among others. *Realism* and *a new realism* as used in these modern contexts refer not to the conventions of a highly illusionistic representational art but rather to an art abstracting from reality, to a nonobjective art based on geometric forms, and also to art using its materials in a raw and non-illusionistic state. These directions are usually concerned with changing the viewer's perceptual habits toward works of art by focusing on the immediacy of the work rid of allusions to symbols and prior times and spaces. These concepts are explained in more detail in reference to Malevich, Léger, Robbe-Grillet and others in this chapter. For an illuminating discussion about styles and attitudes of realism in the visual arts see Roman Jakobson's "On Realism in Art," in Ladislav Matejka and Krystyna Pomorska, eds., *Readings in Russian Poetics,* pp. 38-46.

16. José Ortega y Gasset, *The Dehumanization of Art,* p. 5.

17. Renato Poggioli, *Theory of the Avant-Garde,* p. 80.

18. The distinction made here between romanticism and the avant-garde comes from Ortega. However, I do not wish to oversimplify. The relationship between romanticism and the avant-garde is a complicated issue continually open to historical and critical debate. Poggioli, for instance, shows that in some ways romanticism is related to the avant-garde and in other ways not. He goes on to suggest in his *Theory of the Avant-Garde* that questions of popularity and unpopularity are historically relative, that terms like *the public, the people* and *popular art* must be defined, and that the relationship between romanticism and politics must be examined carefully when looked at in reference to the avant-garde.

Poggioli criticizes Ortega's argument about the popularity of the romantic style (p. 50): "Obviously Ortega too easily identifies the concept of the people with that of the public, as many romantics had also done. The confusion originates from the fact that, while the public for classical art was the aristocracy, the public for modern art (for social and political rather than aesthetic reasons) was becoming and has become an advanced wing of the petty bourgeoisie."

Granting the impossibility of defining romanticism absolutely as the first avant-garde movement, Poggioli summarizes the delicate balance needed to bring the avant-garde and romanticism into legitimate relationship (p. 52): "Whereas the classical tradition is, by definition, one in which there exists no avant-garde force at all, romanticism is—in a certain way and up to a certain point—potential avant-gardism. If such a claim appears excessive, the hypothesis of historical continuity between romanticism and avant-gardism now seems irrefutable: there is not the shadow of a doubt that the latter would have been historically inconceivable without the romantic precedent."

NOTES

19. T.E. Hulme, *Speculations*, pp. 113-40.

20. See P. Adams Sitney, "The Idea of Morphology."

21. For one attempt at a general definition of modernism see Ihab Hassan, "POSTmodernISM."

22. Modernism is defined by friends and foes to suit their respective needs. It is a massive concept which one can culturally limit to the arts or enlarge to take in political and social institutions as well. As definitions vary so much, some have difficulty including in modernism certain philosophical positions and art movements such as German expressionism. Thus I have tried to define that part to which I am referring under formal concerns quite carefully so as not to over-generalize and confuse.

Post-modernism is also difficult to define, but for some different reasons. First, it is new-born and just starting to evolve. I personally place its beginnings at the break-up of minimal art. Following minimalism is process art which destroys the totally enclosed object, conceptualism which looks for other than formal definitions of art and gradually forces out new art issues, performance art and other recent manifestations, all of which question the limits of an abstract art and the place and goals of contemporary art in relation to other institutions. With post-modernism, questions about representation and narrative can be introduced, now totally changed by the critical activities of earlier modernism. See later in chapter 2 for further discussion of the break-up of modernism and the beginnings of post-modernism.

23. George Kubler, *The Shape of Time*, pp. 69-70.

24. Clive Bell, *Art*, pp. 17-18.

25. While Fry subscribes to both significant form and aesthetic emotion and often falls into the pitfalls set up by Bell, he believes that form involves more than just line, colour and space, but also deals with other ideas. See, for instance, "Retrospect," in *Vision and Design*, pp. 284-302.

26. Bell, pp. 149-50.

27. Ibid., p. 45.

28. Fry, p. 72.

29. Clement Greenberg, "Modernist Painting," pp. 103-04.

30. Greenberg, "Necessity of 'Formalism,'" pp. 173-74.

31. Greenberg, *Avant-Garde Attitudes,* p. 10. See also "Problems of Criticism II."

32. Greenberg opposed any form of an intellectual art, extolling inspiration and quality instead, and reducing form to artisanry. He recognized a profound cultural connection between the roots of modernist art and modern science, though he argued that scientific method had no effect on aesthetic quality. The New Critics regarded science as an adversary. They saw a need to rescue the aesthetic and claimed the existence of a particular kind of knowledge peculiar to the language of poetry and quite unlike what could be attained by science.

To anticipate a quite legitimate question: Is it not a contradiction that Greenberg opposes all intellectual art, including the work of Duchamp, Dadaism, conceptualism and, I would most certainly add, minimalism, while he speaks of the self-criticism of an art medium, for is the self-critical act not an intellectual one?

Briefly, Greenberg is concerned with traditional art forms, most especially painting, so that his self-criticism finally becomes merely a technical device for whittling painting down to the "purity" of its physical aspects of paint, canvas and shape. He distorts an intellectual position for his own purposes when he makes an analogy between modernist art and scientific method, arguing for

151

scientific consistency in art by confining visual art to visual experience. The notion that form is a facet of artisanry and that good form is the result of inspiration and good taste is anti-intellectualism disguised as Kantian thought. Greenberg must denigrate new media as "novelty" art because he wants to maintain a continuity between present and past art. Discontinuity, for him, is taboo for it allows for the challenges of an art like conceptualism which often abjures the visual for the written, or minimalism which relies on a priori decision-making and industrial working procedures, including prefabrication, in the composition of its objects.

33. See Murray Krieger, *The New Apologists for Poetry*; Robert Wooster Stallman, "The New Critics" (1947), in *Critiques and Essays in Criticism: 1920-1948*, pp. 488-506; John Crowe Ranson, *The World's Body* and *The New Criticism*; Cleanth Brooks, *The Well Wrought Urn* and *Modern Poetry and the Tradition*; and Allen Tate, *Reason in Madness*.

34. Terence Hawkes, "Conclusions: New 'New Criticism' for Old 'New Criticism'?" in *Structuralism and Semiotics*, especially pp. 155-56.

35. Krieger, p. 5.

36. P. 365.

37. Kasimir Malevich named the movement in painting which he began to work out in 1913 suprematism. In 1919 he proclaimed it at an end. He was its prime proponent, with followers such as Ivan Puni and Ivan Kliun. Suprematism was influenced by Cézanne and much more by the cubism of Picasso and Braque. Yet suprematism was more radical than cubism. Cubism abstracted from depicted reality, fragmenting its representations into various geometric patterns for resulting simultaneous views, flattening spaces in the course of rejecting transparency and conventional illusionism, enclosing the object as object of art separate from other objects. Yet suprematism went further. Malevich painted in a cubo-futurist style before theorizing about and working in the movement he named. He spoke of a nonobjective art, an art not derived, as was cubism, from a pre-existing object or situation but one based only on colour and geometric form. The minimal elements used created spatial and colour studies detached more thoroughly than cubism from representation and illusionism. Suprematism left its influence on Soviet constructivism with Vladimir Tatlin, Alexander Rodchenko, Liubov Popova, Alexander Vesnin and others.

38. Kasimir Malevich, *Essays on Art*, 2 vols. Page numbers of references to this source will be given in the text.

39. Ortega y Gassett, p. 23.

40. Lee T. Lemon and Marion J. Reis, trans., *Russian Formalist Criticism*, p. 112. Both Shklovsky essays, "Sterne's *Tristram Shandy*" and "Art as Technique," along with Eichenbaum's "The Theory of the 'Formal Method'" are from this source.

41. Ibid., pp. 115-22.

42. *The Life and Opinions of Tristram Shandy* appeared in nine volumes from 1760 to 1767. It was a great success in its time. It is remarkable because it totally defies the developing form of the eighteenth-century novel which was Aristotelian in its linearity and causality. *Tristram Shandy* is sometimes called the first philosophical novel as well as the first psychological novel, anticipating in its radical form the work of James Joyce and other twentieth-century writers. It uses notions from John Locke's *Essay on Human Understanding* in terms of associations of ideas, stream of consciousness and the relativity of time.

NOTES

43. Shklovsky, "Sterne's *Tristram Shandy*," in Lemon and Reis, p. 57.

44. Shklovsky, "Art as Technique," in Lemon and Reis, p. 12.

45. Shklovsky, "Sterne's *Tristram Shandy*, in Lemon and Reis, p. 27.

46. Ibid., p. 31.

47. René Wellek and Austin Warren, *Theory of Literature*, p. 232.

48. Quoted in Eichenbaum, "The Theory of the 'Formal Method,'" in Lemon and Reis, p. 118.

49. Lewis Jacobs, ed., *Introduction to the Art of the Movies*, pp. 96-98.

50. Alain Robbe-Grillet, *For a New Novel*, p. 12.

51. Ibid., p. 155.

52. Ibid., p. 159.

53. Ibid., p. 161.

54. Shklovsky, "Art as Technique," in Lemon and Reis, p. 24.

55. Morse Peckham, *Man's Rage for Chaos*, p. xi.

56. Ibid., pp. 211-12.

57. Ibid., p. 218.

58. Ibid., p. 68.

59. Morse Peckham, *Art and Pornography*, p. 114.

60. Ibid.

61. Ibid., p. 220.

62. Ibid., p. 162.

Chapter 3

1. Pierre Thebérge, ed., *About 30 Works by Michael Snow*, p. 21.

2. Brydon Smith, ed., *Michael Snow/Canada*, p. 25.

3. Ibid., p. 29. See also Appendix C for text.

4. Ibid.

5. Amy Taubin, "Doubled Visions," p. 42.

6. The subtitle of *Painting*, which is *Closing the Drum Book*, has several significant references. A drummer friend named Larry Dubin once gave Snow a book called *The Drum Book*. From it Snow later abstracted a page illustrating drums. He called the resulting painting of 1960 *The Drumbook*. Snow's friendship with the drummer continued and they were both playing—Snow on piano and trumpet—in the jazz improvisational group CCMC in Toronto when Dubin died suddenly in the spring of 1978, two days before the band was to leave for a European tour.

Chapter 4

1. *Skvoz' Literaturu* (Leningrad, 1924), p. 236, and quoted in Victor Erlich, *Russian Formalism*, p. 254.

2. An example of a film with a mythopoetic structure is *Dog Star Man*. For

heavily psychological and myth-making attitudes in his writing see *The Brakhage Lectures*.

3. Stan Brakhage, *Metaphors on Vision*. The entire Fall 1963 issue of *Film Culture* is given over to Brakhage and carries this title.

4. See *Metaphors on Vision*; also "Part Two: On Splicing" from *A Moving Picture Giving and Taking Book*, pp. 23-40. "On Splicing" first appeared in *Film Culture*, no. 35 (Winter 1964-65), pp. 51-56, and later as Part II of "A Moving Picture Giving and Taking Book," *Film Culture*, no. 41 (Summer 1966), pp. 46-50.

5. See "The Camera Eye" and "My Eye" in *Metaphors on Vision*, no pagination; also a paragraph by Brakhage quoted by Annette Michelson in "Film and the Radical Aspiration," pp. 40-41.

6. Stephen Koch, *Stargazer*, p. 39; and P. Adams Sitney, *Visionary Film*, pp. 410-11. Both Koch and Sitney give certain little-known facts about Warhol's working procedures.

7. Jonas Mekas, "Sixth Independent Film Award."

8. Andrée Hayum, "Information or Illusion," p. 58.

9. Ibid.

10. See Appendix B for poem and credits.

11. This final segment became *Encyclopaedia* (1965), a work in ink on printed paper, 96" x 48".

12. Quoted in Calvin Tomkins, *The Bride and the Bachelors*, p. 97.

13. Michael Snow, "Letter," p. 4.

14. Ibid., p. 1.

15. Ibid., p. 3.

16. Lawrence Alloway, "Systemic Painting," introductory essay in *Systemic Painting*, a catalogue for a show organized by Alloway at the Guggenheim Museum (New York, 1966) and reprinted in *Minimal Art*, p. 38.

17. Ibid., p. 55.

18. In addition to Snow's own description and my elaboration of it, I should like to call the reader's attention to descriptions of *Wavelength* by four other writers. Perhaps the most notable is that of Manny Farber who calls it "a straightforward document of a room in which a dozen businesses have lived and gone bankrupt," in *Negative Space*, p. 250. There is also Annette Michelson, "Toward Snow: Part I." Her description is combined with a partial phenomenological analysis of the film. Another appears in P. Adams Sitney's "Structural Film," p. 4, anthologized in slightly revised form in *Film Culture Reader*, pp. 332-33, and in a still further revised version in his *Visionary Film*. Finally there is Gene Youngblood's *Expanded Cinema*, pp. 122-27. Youngblood's description is quite interesting. It should be noted that in spite of all the rhetoric about the simplification of shape in *Wavelength* and other so-called structural films, P. Adams Sitney in the first two versions of his essay and Gene Youngblood in his book both err in their descriptions of events in Snow's film.

19. It seems appropriate here to distinguish between the terms *serial*, *series* and *variation*. John Coplans in *Serial Imagery*, pp. 10-11, writes:

> Serial Imagery is a type of repeated form or structure shared equally by each work in a group of related works made by one artist. To paint in series, however, is not necessarily to be Serial. Neither the number of works nor

the similarity of theme in a given series determines whether a painting or sculpture is Serial. Rather, Seriality is identified by a particular inter-relationship, rigorously consistent, of structure and syntax: Serial structures are produced by a single indivisible process that links the internal structure of a work to that of other works within a differentiated whole. While a Series may have any number of works, it must, as a precondition of Seriality, have at least two. Thus a uniquely conceived painting or sculpture cannot be Serial.

He goes on to explain that seriality and serial structure are distinguished by a macro-structure, and that series "refers to a more simple grouping of forms in any kind of set" (p 19).

Elsewhere (*Andy Warhol*, p. 49) Coplans explains that serial forms are also different from the concept of theme and variation. "In the latter, the structure may be the same, but the composition is sufficiently varied so that each painting, though belonging to a set, can be recognized as unique." Seriality uses repetition and redundancy and has nothing to do with notions of uniqueness and masterpieces. He comments further that the serial works have no hierarchies of meaning or rank, and can be added to indefinitely, the choice of this last dependent upon the artist and the system he determines to employ.

See also Lawrence Alloway, "Serial Forms," in *American Sculpture of the Sixties*, ed. Maurice Tuchman, pp. 14-15.

20. Alloway, "Systemic Painting," p. 45.

21. Michael Snow, "Passage."

22. Joseph V. Mascelli and Arthur Miller, eds., *American Cinematographer Manual*, p. 204.

23. See Noël Burch's systematic attempt to deal with space in chapters 1 and 2 of his *Theory of Film Practice*, pp. 3-31. Burch stresses the importance of off-screen space.

24. Erwin Panofsky, "Style and Medium in the Motion Pictures," p. 18.

25. Noël Burch and Jorge Dana attribute the phrase "space as limit and space as milieu" to Focillon in their essay "Propositions," p. 44.

26. In his further revised essay "Structural Film," now in his book *Visionary Film*, P. Adams Sitney writes, referring to structural film: "Since the middle sixties a number of filmmakers have emerged whose approach is quite different, although dialectically related to the sensibility of their predecessors. Michael Snow, George Landow, Hollis Frampton, Paul Sharits, Tony Conrad, Ernie Gehr, and Joyce Wieland have produced a number of remarkable films apparently in the opposite direction of that formal thrust. Theirs is a cinema of structure in which the shape of the whole is predetermined and simplified, and it is that shape which is the primal impression of the film."

Such older works by filmmakers such as Markopoulos, Peterson, Anger, Brakhage and Kubelka moved "toward increased cinematic complexity," according to Sitney, who continues: "A precise statement of the difference between formal and structural organization must involve a sense of the working process; the formal film is a tight nexus of content, a shape designed to explore facets of the material. . . . Recurrences, prolepses, antitheses, and overall rhythms are the rhetoric of the formal; in its highest form, the content of such films would be a mythic encounter" (p. 407).

He says, further on, "The structural film insists on its shape, and what content it has is minimal and subsidiary to the outline." He then states the four characteristics of the structural film: a "fixed camera position (fixed frame from the viewer's perspective), the flicker effect, loop printing and rephotography off the screen" (pp. 407-08).

Sitney's questionable and controversial label causes considerable confusion

155

and has nothing to do with structuralism as a methodology of linguistics and the social sciences. His description raises more questions than it clarifies. Structure, according to Sitney, is shape, and form is something else. Earlier film is complex. Structural film has a predetermined and simplified shape and minimal content. All is subsidiary to its outline. The formal film explores facets of its materials, and "in its highest form its content would be mythic." But what precisely are its materials—the mythic content or the rhetorical devices? It seems pertinent to raise these questions here for Sitney's often quoted and little analyzed terminology brings one directly to *Wavelength*. In the same chapter he describes Snow as the "dean of structural film-makers," adding that "*Wavelength* may be the supreme achievement of the form." Elsewhere, Sitney says that Snow's film became the inspiration for this new category—that of the structural film, placing importance as well as an unsolicited burden on *Wavelength*.

What occurs with this terminology is that Sitney seems explicitly to deny that such film as he calls "structural," including Snow's work from *Wavelength* through *Side Seat Slides Paintings Sound Film* and *Breakfast*, a.k.a. *Table Top Dolly*, is formal, and through his vocabulary calls it simplified as opposed to the "increased complexity" of earlier work. In this way he implicitly denigrates it. On the other hand he defines formal rhetoric as "recurrences, prolepses, antitheses, and overall rhythms." But surely the flicker film and the loop are both marked by recurrences and *Wavelength* has all four rhetorical means. This is a strange notion of formal devices and an odd way of leaving out the so-called structural film. Sitney's language is carelessly used at times. "Mythic encounter" is part of the rhetoric he employs in positing a romantic aesthetic for the American avant-garde.

But he also generates other problems. Is he not suggesting that structural film is merely about devices and the use of devices? So that even while he separates structural from formal film, is he not equating structural film in a pejorative sense with the formalism of Greenberg or Bell? He maintains that structural film has little or no content. For Sitney the words *formal* and *content* imply the complex, while his use of *minimal* suggests less than complex, thus less qualitatively. This is an attitude held by those romantic and expressionistic advocates of earlier American art against minimalism and one also carried over now against conceptual art. This implies that there is less to perceive, less to deal with on the part of the viewer. Preconception, choice, decision, attitude toward making are left out of consideration in favour of concern with traces of making, autobiographical gesture, mythopoetic and other ironic goals. This denigration of minimalism ignores the relationship or transaction between perceiver and object, and the increased demands placed on the viewer, that include the active means of constituting the art so much a concern of the various visual arts and literature.

Chapter 5

1. Brakhage's work since at least the Pittsburgh trilogy of films—*Eyes* (1970), *Deux Ex* and *The Act of Seeing with One's Own Eyes* (both 1971)—appears less involved with psychology and mythology.

2. In response to a question posed by P. Adams Sitney in his interview with Brakhage at the beginning of *Metaphors on Vision* in *Film Culture*, no. 30, no pagination.

3. "The Life and Times of Michael Snow," *Take One* 3, no. 3 (January-February 1971; published April 7, 1972), p. 10.

4. *Film-Makers' Cooperative Catalogue No. 5*, p. 300.

5. Pierre Théberge, *About 30 Works by Michael Snow*, p. 25.

6. In *About 30 Works* Théberge comments: "The autobiographical content of *Sink* may account for its relatively small, intimate scale" (p. 27).

7. Ibid.

8. Brydon Smith, ed., *Michael Snow/Canada*, p. 31.

9. Théberge, p. 19.

10. This description of *Two Sides to Every Story* and the accompanying discussion of description and literalization appear in slightly different form in "Michael Snow" by this author, in *Projected Images*, pp. 26-33.

11. This description is an edited version of "Michael Snow: *Cover to Cover* and Back . . ." by this author.

12. See Susan Sontag's discussion of doubling in "Spiritual Style in the Films of Robert Bresson," in *Against Interpretation*, pp. 181-198. She writes: "The typical way in which 'form' shapes 'content' in art is by doubling, duplicating. Symmetry and repetition of motifs in painting, the double plot in Elizabethan drama, and rhyme schemes in poetry are a few obvious examples" (p. 183). And, more specifically, speaking of Bresson's narration she writes: "But, more interestingly, it often doesn't tell us anything we don't know or are about to learn. It 'doubles' the action. In this case, we usually get the word first, then the scene" (p. 186).

Chapter 6

1. *Film Culture*, no. 46, p. 3.

2. *Film Culture*, nos. 48-49 (Winter and Spring 1970), p. 11.

3. *Film Culture*, no. 46, p.4.

4. Michael Fried, *Three American Painters*, p. 40.

5. *Film Culture*, no. 46, p. 4.

6. *Take One* 3, no. 3, p. 10.

7. *Film Culture*, no. 46, p. 4.

8. The reader is referred to Freytag's Pyramid based on a five-act play construction and named after Gustav Freytag in the mid-nineteenth century. Originally he took his model from the structure of tragedy, but it is present in other dramatic and literary forms such as comedy, melodrama, the novel and short story, to say nothing of the adaptations of these on film. The parts are: introduction or exposition; rising action or complication; climax; falling action or reversal; and denouement or unraveling. In tragedy, properly speaking, catastrophe is used rather than denouement. In many forms falling action and denouement are often used synonymously, as I have done in this discussion.

9. Manny Farber, *Negative Space*, p. 258.

10. T.E. Hulme, *Speculations*, p. 126.

11. Alain Robbe-Grillet, *For a New Novel*, p. 70.

Chapter 7

1. Michael Snow, "*La Région Centrale*," pp. 60, 62.

2. Jonas Mekas, "Movie Journal."

3. *Film Culture*, no. 52, p. 58.

4. Ibid., p. 62.

5. All told the 190-minute film cost $27,000. Snow was assisted by a Canadian Film Development Corporation Grant and also an "investment" from Famous Players in Toronto.

6. "Michael Snow's *La Région Centrale*," *Artforum* 12, no. 3, p. 67. See also Locke's second part with the same title in *Artforum* 12, no. 4.

7. *Film Culture*, no. 52, p. 58.

8. Ibid., p. 60.

9. John Locke uses the term "frame movement" in his November 1973 *Artforum* article (see particularly note 5, p. 71) to include actual camera movement and the appearance of movement.

10. Michael Fried, *Three American Painters*, p. 11.

11. Pierre Théberge, *About 30 Works by Michael Snow*, p. 35.

12. *Film Culture*, no. 52, p. 58.

13. Théberge, pp. 35, 33.

14. "The Camera and the Spectator: Michael Snow in Discussion with John DuCane," p. 197; and in "Michael Snow in Conversation with John DuCane," in *Light*.

15. *Film Culture*, no. 52, p. 63.

16. Ibid., p. 61.

17. But in a later work the "bodies" can be included in another example of new art made from old. *De La* now exists exclusively as a video installation, the technology having been redesigned to accommodate a video camera and four video monitors, one in each corner of a space, with the camera from *La Région Centrale* mounted on its machine in the centre. As in *La Région Centrale* and in contrast to *Authorization*, the machinery never records itself. One can watch *De La* as it records the surroundings as well as watch the surroundings themselves, the electronic representation on one or more of the four monitors, and be personally included in all the processes of presentation and representation.

18. Alain Robbe-Grillet, *For a New Novel*, pp. 65, 73. Page numbers of all subsequent quotations from this work will be given in the text.

Chapter 8

1. Bill Auchterlone, "Review—Artfilms," p. 48.

2. "Michael Snow in Conversation with John DuCane."

3. Michael Snow, "Passage."

4. Herbert Josephs, *Diderot's Dialogue of Language and Gesture*. See "Dédoublement and Dialogue," pp. 84-103.

5. Denis Diderot, *Rameau's Nephew and Other Works*, pp. 86-87.

6. These two Snow quotations are reprinted in program notes for *"Rameau's Nephew"*. . . for the Twenty-ninth Edinburgh Film Festival, 1975.

7. See Michael Fried, "Toward a Supreme Fiction." Fried discusses Diderot's idea about the tableau in theatre and painting. One can see seeds of the

argument for Diderot as precursor of modernism in Fried's discussion. Note also Richard Sennett, "Diderot's Paradox of Acting," in chapter 2, pp. 110-15, of *The Fall of Public Man*, on signs of the performance, artifice, gesture, and Diderot's notion of emotion as presentation in acting; and Herbert Josephs, *Diderot's Dialogue of Language and Gesture*.

8. Letter to Mekas, *Village Voice*, February 3, 1975. Edinburgh notes, p. 4 (see n. 6, above).

9. Fried, "Toward a Supreme Fiction." Diderot speaks of both in his *Lettre sur les sourds et muets* to which Fried refers. The quotation is from and by Fried, p. 567, n. 45.

10. Josephs, pp. 84-103.

11. Jonas Mekas, *Village Voice*, December 16, 1974. Edinburgh notes, p. 3 (see n. 6 above).

12. Fried, "Toward a Supreme Fiction," especially pp. 553-55, 566-67, 570-75, 579; also Josephs.

13. Samuel Beckett used a similar device in *Play,* in which characters speak as a spotlight hits them.

Appendix A

The following is an unpublished text. Punctuation, spelling and emphasis follow the original. W.W. is Snow's abbreviation for the Walking Woman.

"A Lot of Near Mrs."   Michael Snow 1962-63 Toronto-New York

Closed shop. Trade*mark*. Trade: Art. *A* sign *to* sign. Put the outside inside where it belongs. Simultaneity. "She" is the same in different places and different times at same place and time. Repetition: Trademark, my trade, my mark. Mock mass production. Art the only 'cottage industry' left. Juxtaposition: a "surrealism" of media within one subject. Social comment, narrative, realism, satire, allegory, abstraction, didacticism, mysticism: art from drawing to past sculpture. Stage director. Fact and fiction: the relationships between space and light illusions (imagination?) and a physically finite object. Coloring books: anyone can do it. Jane Arden. Perils of Pauline. W.W. is detached from her background or "she" is in reciprocal relations to it. If "she" is cut-out (no depicted background) alone on the wall the relationships might be just internal or just with the real environment. Art as a form of *mumm*ification. "Solid color space ladies." Women historically as subject in art. Women "characters", "types," "actresses" designed by artists. Cranach, Rubens, Ingres, Renoir, Pascin, Modigliani, Picasso etc. "Abstract" *this* element of painting. *One* drawing. Contour to be not only rectangle but just contour of single subject. To "cut-out" means to (slang) leave. Girl watching. Passing out of the picture and yes we'll soon be passing out of the picture. Pedestrienne. Stepping out. Yes my work is pedestrian. Revelation of process as subject in Pollock, DeKooning continue. Scientific method. Experiments. Problem of originality: invent a subject. Impossible but try. Presence-absence. Be a *tracer of missing persons*. The subject could have been *my* image but prefer to add, multiply create not mirror. Use time: outdoor exposure for one month: weather woman Jan. 1 to 31. Weather report. Given *model* tracing, stenciling, printing are means of including the subject in the work, in the process show the path of the model. My subject is not women or a woman *but* the first cardboard cutout of W.W. I made. A second remove depiction. Always use it same size as original. 5 ft. tall. W.W. is not an idea, its just a drawing, not a very good one either! Bad taste conversion W.W. though representational is invented, an *individual*. One subject, *any* medium. My work is *inclusive* not exclusive, puppetry, choreography. I'm not so interested in making a lot of paintings, sculpture etc. as finding out what happens when you do such and such a thing. A stand-in or abstract person. Attempt to extend certain values of American abstract painting by doing them backwards or "wrong"(?). "Art" and "life" problem. Duchamp. If you can use stuff from the street as art in an art gallery why can't you use "paintings" or art as art in the street. Not found art but *lost* art. Who can see it? Trying to find new uses for representation. Not a "figure painter." Abstraction of *style*. Is that possible? But art is something too. What? An "abstract" shape can be sexier than a (beautiful) representation of a (beautiful) breast but neither are sexier than a (beautiful) breast. Art is an addition to life not only a quote. If you can use "anything" to make art how about a self contained factory where the material is made to make the art with. What if Braque had printed his own newspaper to use in his collages. I'm doing that. Exhibition "announcements" as much part of it as the paintings All art. Figure in art: "poses" have been explored (Rodin) no more poses. "New" representational art and its uses. A representation can be used for something else. I will take orders for any use to which "she" might be put. *Art pimp*. Lady fence, lady table, lady chair, lady lamp, rubber (balloon) lady, water bottle lady, fur lady, stained glass lady, lady road sign, lady shovel, lady car, lady dart board, lady hat rack, leading lady, first lady, lady like. Home made ready made, ways to maintain the freedom of color possible in abstract painting, represent a woman and not be surrealist ie., look a green woman! Space must not be 'deep' color and form, material must be one, if any, brush strokes must be subordinate to the image. Art is artificial, not life-like, not warm. Food art goes bad. For me superiority of Vermeer to Rembrandt and of Rembrandts drawing to his paintings...myth Canada, myth America, modern myth. What are the differences in "meaning" in comparing the same form (W.W.) in sponge rubber, in plastic, in sand, in light, etc.?* Forms made by manipulation of material, what happens when there is an image on or in the material. Little paintings, printings in street, subway, etc. Compositions of same. Perhaps another painter might paint it. Audience participation: people scribble on, attack etc. These "posters," who thinks they are "art"? I've reclaimed some of the drawn-on etc. ones. Dispersal: 4 or 5 "paintings" in the street, related but separated by as many blocks. Valery: "The subject of a poem is as foreign to it and as important, as his name is to a man." Influences and thank you: Duchamp, Matisse, DeKooning, Mondrian. Echoings of artists working in "Happenings" and "environments," the ideas, having never seen same. Personality could that be a subject? Patent pending. reaction painter. Culturally today anyone who doesn't know jazz (AM Negro music) doesn't know their arts from a hole in the ground. I'm optically amoral. I don't see what those signs and those things are selling. Some of my ideas turn out to be similar. An unexplainable coincidence which is not leading me to work directly from that material tho I often see signs, displays, etc., which are very interesting. I like work of Johns, Oldenberg, Dine, partly because apparently they came to similar conclusions arising out of the accomplishments of the great senior New York painters. Media scale: sculpture, relief, painting, drawing, printing, film, music. I arbitrarily continue with an arbitrarily chosen subject: It was not designed for uses which could be foreseen. Chance. I take a chance"drawn personification" of things that happened in abstract art. Tatooing. Art as art criticism (reversible). Opposites. Film I'm working on seems to concern itself with the poetry of the juxtaposition of the static and the dynamic, absence, presence, development of events-for-capture = art series of photographs taken in Toronto April '62. Setting a plywood black cut-out of W.W. in street and recording passerby reaction and often beautiful resulting compositions. Neurotic, erotic, aesthetic. Make light of the figure. Made first cut-out or wall life size "realistic" figures of cardboard in Oct. 1960. They were result of several years worrying about *where* the figure is or could be

161

or would be. This is the problem. I solved it by removing the figure from *where* and putting it *here*. On the wall or in the room. She was detached from her background or removed from her "environment" and placed in a "foreign" one. In painting a figure on/in the rectangle the relationships exist between the figure and its environment. When you paint a 'cut-out' flat representation of a figure rather than on a rectangle, the relationships now are internal. The 'environment' of the figure now becomes separate, and out of my control. But now I think of where as well as what. ("lost" compositions, mail, females, publicity pix, etc.). No distortions of figure itself. W.W. always same contour. I *don't "believe"* in representation. But we really look and say "it's a woman!" Passing through. Is "material" a representation too. Is it any *realer*. We *must* believe that it is. My "subject" is the same in the 59 and 60 abstract paintings and sculpture but now it is acted. Time. Impossible. La Femme qui Marche. Near miss. Women are the nearest "other". The first "other". There is something *inside* repetition. "Participation mystique" with machine production. Hand made art-machine made art. Detachiste art. Tits and arts.

Appendix B

Prologue and Music Credits for
New York Eye and Ear Control

The woman will be thrown at the woods,
closed down in a padded coaming by men
who handle their attachments with runcible
spoons, and you will then be satisfied,
for men in woods and audiences, chosen
for their slowheartedness, are perpetuities
insisted on in the strain of her passage,
goaded in bah relief and pried from the
drip pans of reputation.

Prologue written by Paul Haines.

Music by: Albert Ayler, Don Cherry, John Tchicai, Roswell Rudd,
Gary Peacock, Sonny Murray.

Appendix C

The following is Part Three, the text of *Tap*, 1969. Spelling and punctuation follow Snow's original.

The "drumming" sound which you have heard, are hearing, will hear or perhaps won't ever hear I made by tapping my fingers against a microphone while moving it over the tape recorder to make a bit of feedback. I then made a loop of a selection from the resulting tape. There is a large blowup of a photograph of the above procedure which you may have seen or will see etc. It's supposed to be hanging somewhere in this building. The tape and the photo were made in February 1969 and this is being taped on March 14, 1969. Joyce Wieland Snow and I took the photos with a Miranda 35 mm camera, an 8" x 10" print from the selected negative was made by "Modernage" on 48th Street and the 6' x 40" blowup was made by "Independent" on 48th Street. It cost $36.00.

I wanted to make a composition which was dispersed, in which the elements would be come upon in different ways and which would consist of 1. a sound, 2. an image, 3. a text, 4. an object, 5. a line, which would be unified but the parts of which would be of interest in themselves if the connections between them were not seen (but better if seen). One of many additional considerations was that it be partly tactile, body made tho using machines. Typewriting is a very similar finger tapping to the way the tape was made and I thought that perhaps I should make a complementary object by finger tapping but finally decided to show the loudspeaker as the object, as a "found" element which spreads the "created" element. The speaker is just a cheap portable speaker I got about five years ago and I considered "including" it more by painting it, perhaps I will, at this writing it is dark brown, its original color. Rather than change the "given" color of the speaker or its shape I decided to continue the color. This and the photo are black and white and the wire is black. Since the brown speaker "frames" the sound I used the same brown in framing both this and the photo. The frames are also rectangular "loops". The line, which of course, properly speaking is also an object I decided to compose through whatever building the place is in. It partly "composes" itself according to its own nature but it eventually "disappears" to the tape recorder which is now (?) playing the tape so that it (the wire) has a "spread" which in its own terms has some similarity to the acoustical spacial spread of the sound, eventually disappearing. I decided against showing the playback tape recorder because the source of the sound at this time and historically is here described and in the photo, pictured. In a sense the black line (carrier of the sound)disappears to here (text) to the photograph (image) both of which are "traces" of it and to the actual (hidden) tape recorder.

This piece is an attempt to, among other things, do something manipulative with memory devices: tape recorder, camera, typewriter. It is *not* a "mixed-media" or collage-assemblage piece, nor is it theatre. As is proper to the use of the above devices I've attempted to use memory as an aspect of the work. I have made separated or "dispersed" compositions since 1961, some of them having parts on

164

different continents but with the exception of certain performance pieces (eg. "Right Reader" 1965) and films (simultaneous in elements and site) the parts were always in the same medium, involved, images only (if that's possible) or worked in an image to object scale.

"Tap" is a kind of still sound movie. The ways in which the different elements occupy space are interesting: The sound filling it, having a source but no definite "edges" the line, reading backwards, threading and carrying the sound and having an unseen end, the image flat, two dimensional, this flat, black, linear, small, in your eyes and in your mind.

Appendix D

Description by sequence of Michael Snow's *"Rameau's Nephew"* *by Diderot (Thanx to Dennis Young) by Wilma Schoen* (1973-74)

The following is a description of each of the twenty-five parts, fragments, sections, tableaux, all referred to here simply as sequences. Sequences 1 through 4 can be viewed as the Preface; 5 through 22 as the body of the text, with the Signature, Erratum and Addendum following.

A section of patterns of solid colour images appears before each sequence in the main body of the work, although not in the Preface nor after the main part. These sections of colour patterns are referred to here and in chapter 8 as anacruses, and function as visual analogues for musical and literary equivalents. They act as rests, while they also often code the colours of clothing or of translucent filters to be anticipated within the next sequence. The patterns of colour change vary from slow and gentle to quasi flicker-like rhythms.

An earlier description was written by Margie Keller as an appendix to her program notes used for a viewing of the film on May 30, 1975 at the Film Center of the Art Institute of Chicago. The following description is substantially longer and corrects a number of technical and other inaccuracies.

1. Michael Snow whistling. Snow whistles into a microphone. He stands head and shoulders against a red background for a frontal, a side and a back view.

2. "FOCUS." The word appears in and out of focus and later jiggles in the frame. In the background a Beatles song is audible and is quickly tuned out, replaced by a voice-over giving biographical information in French and then in German on Jean-Philippe Rameau. Whistling trails off into the next sequence.

3. Woman at piano. A woman, Michael Snow's mother, sits at a piano and addressing the audience, recites biographical information on Rameau in Spanish.

4. Credits. They appear on the screen as they are also read in voice-over by a man with a pronounced stutter who is sometimes corrected by Snow as he proceeds. The subtitle reads: "For English Speaking Audiences Only." It is "Based on the Decameron by Boccaccio and the 'Bhagavad Gita'" and "Dedicated to Alexander Graham Bell." This is followed by grant acknowledgements. Then a cast of more than 150 individual and company names rolls upward and is superimposed over a leftward moving train. Of the more than 150 names, nearly three dozen are anagrams of Michael Snow.

5. Mental Profumo L'Alito. A small mint tin the size of a pocket aspirin container is turned over to read "Mental Profumo L'Alito" on its front. There is no sound.

6. Office scene. An office scene with Jonas Mekas and two other people as they try to locate the source of a voice in various objects in the room. The image finally falls down and out of frame, as the voices are heard trailing off as well.

7. Airplane. Five people appear in this sequence, including Alfie, a loquacious boy of about ten. They discuss tea, food and a range of banal subjects rife with clichés as the camera moves in patterns—horizontal pans, tilts, diagonals, intricately and abruptly cutting on syllables, words, phrases and sentences from speaker to speaker to various parts of the plane. At times the image is cut at an angle and gradually cut per cut arched around in circular movements or simply turns in a continuous circle as it seems to defy gravity; one thinks of *La Région Centrale* and at times ◄———►. Plane and engine sounds are heard. Using the principle of the Doppler Effect voices rise and drop in pitch and volume, sometimes making voices at either extreme of volume unintelligible. Lines are repeated and requoted. There is punning on plain and plane sound along with ideas about time. Colour transparencies are used here. *For* and its homonyms are counted and registered through numbers on the screen. The sequence begins with "Quote" and ends with "Unquote." Before the cast appears Snow is heard in voice-over: "I may be putting words into your mouth but . . ." And then later he is heard dictating lines to his performers.

8. Sink. Hands, those of Snow himself, drum in an empty kitchen sink which is then filled with water and emptied again. The drumming concludes when the sink is again empty.

9. Dennis Burton. In a gaming form of logomachy, painter Dennis Burton sits at a desk in a white suit facing the audience and reads a text. On certain percussive consonant sounds and at certain volumes his video image is interfered with by colour patterns. Burton's private speech is virtually undecipherable until near the end of the sequence when Snow off-screen asks him a question to which Burton responds affirmatively, repeating Snow's statement, thereby revealing to the audience the method of his game.

10. A loft. People sit at a table or stand about with scripts in hand. Against the back wall is a tape recorder and a record player. There is a typewriter on the table together with fruit and other food and a telephone on the side. The scene is repeated three times, with additions and variations. The first time it is read live from scripts with harpsicord music by Rameau being played on the record player. This is being taped. The second time the tape is played back as it is mimed by the participants and new verbal and other material is added, including bells, telephones and more music. The third time the first two tapes are played back, more new verbal material is read from the script and more harpsicord music is presented. A quasi-flicker film, the same as appears on the anacrusis prior to this sequence, is reprojected three separate times, each time from a different position or point of view. A sheet of green acetate appears and is moved to various parts of the room. People change records, talk on the phone, kiss, laugh, pun. *To's* and their homonyms are defined while *fors* are again counted. The yellow chair from

Wavelength appears at the end, as a woman, Amy Taubin, stands next to it and makes a phone call. She is the same person who appears at the phone in *Wavelength*, next to the yellow chair.

11. Bus. People sitting in the back of a bus. Camera records them in long shot looking up as if at the voice-over which lectures with a pronounced lisp on man's demand for greater and greater realism and the technological advances in three-dimensional illusionist systems. Meanwhile the image itself is increasingly punctured with pockmarks. There are also flares and end roll dots. Interrupting the lecture a woman's voice, that of Joyce Wieland, the narrator in 16, says, "There are two threes."

12. A tea party. The camera zooms out from the eye of a cameraman at a 16mm camera to reveal two men and two women (one of whom is actress Jackie Burroughs) at tea. A few words are intelligible. The entire sequence is then reversed from end to beginning and more words become intelligible. The actors recite their words and entire sentences backwards so that when repeated from end to beginning (tail to head on the film) one hears words in their proper order (though the backward recording somewhat distorts the words). Homonyms for *for* are again counted through numbers which are held up on the screen. Through the gestures of the actors and their words which can be read forward and backward one understands that they are discussing an unpleasant smell in the room.

13. In front of a mock-up of an Indian village. Four people stand in front of the Indian village mock-up, two women and two men; one of the men, in a bright yellow two-piece suit and a red turban, slightly resembles Ben Turpin. In long, medium and then close-up shots the camera records them mouthing sounds which are not heard, while on the soundtrack one voice begins, "This is really artificial, there's nothing natural about it," and so on.

Animal and other sounds are heard, including thunder, dishes breaking, bells, drum rolls, an explosion. Gradually sounds and images are both distorted, abstracted; the images are rephotographed over and over until they become areas of colour or black and white and the sounds also tampered with are heard as squeaks. At times the image slips as does, apparently, the sound. The entire section is extremely fragmented through the close-ups and rephotographing and distortions of sound.

14. Pissing duet. Snow refers to this as a "pissing duet" with a man and a woman, though it does look more like "a pissing contest between a man and a woman" as Margie Keller has described it. It is placed midway through the film, at a point where one might naturally want to take a break.

15. Embassy. Elegant eighteenth-century rooms become the setting for artist Nam June Paik, critic Annette Michelson, filmmakers Bob Cowan and Helene Kaplan and a woman named Yoko Orimoto, referred to in the film as Alexia, as they perform various voice, breath and speech acts, use puns and clichés and execute other gestures, often puppet-like. Each voice and breath exercise and

each phrase or sentence is spotlighted by a lightman visible within the frame. He and the soundman who is also visible readjust their positions in the frame on each new shot. Michelson lectures on "interesting subjects," with words often including forms of *for* as the homonyms continue to be counted. Bob Dylan's "A Hard Rain's A-Gonna Fall" is played on the cassette recorder, which Paik attempts to learn, and anticipates the rain in sequence 18. The often awkward and comic gestures of the participants stand out in relief here. Their parlour games appear mysterious in the elegant setting.

16. Tabletop description. Stationery, pens, pencils, a roll of 16mm film, 35mm slides, videotape, brushes and other supplies including a typewriter are moved about on a tabletop by a man's hands, those of Snow. A woman, Joyce Wieland, in voice-over narrates the activities, sometimes in sync but often ahead of or behind the movements. The camera remains stationary.

17. TV family. In long shot a man and a woman holding a child seem to be watching television and pointing with amusement in the general direction of the set as one hears laughter on the soundtrack. There is a cut to a close-up of a yellow chair (familiar from *Wavelength*) with a microphone on it as the laughter continues, as if this were the image the family were watching. The camera is stationary in both shots.

18. Woman at window. A woman, Joyce Wieland, stands framed within a window of a log cabin. Rain is heard. Gradually water appears on screen level; finally the water vanishes from the surface and Wieland disappears. One recalls that "A Hard Rain's A-Gonna Fall" by Dylan was on the soundtrack in the embassy sequence. The camera remains stationary throughout.

19. English comedians. In voice-over two English comedians are heard with very strong regional accents extremely difficult to understand, made more difficult by the laughter and applause accompanying their routine. Two men and a woman are present in each of the three shots which occur and recur. Each of the shots is coded to appear on one or another of the comedians' voices or on applause and laughter. Each of the three shots is distinctly lit, two from the side and one from the front. If one listens long enough one might begin to hear the comedians' vague talk about Adam and Eve, God, reincarnation.

20. Cheap hotel suite. A group of people are gathered in hotel rooms. Early on an old man tells a story; on each syllable the camera cuts to another object or person in the room, fragmenting in cubist fashion. Film devices are put at the service of philosophical questions concerning appearance, reality, illusion and technological systems of verisimilitude. The old man is metamorphosed through dissolves into a young one; a superimposed table is not seen by those in the room; sounds are detached from their sources. Puns and clichés abound, also at the service of philosophical questions. "Seeing is believing" is replaced by "touching is believing," "eating is believing," and "hearing is deceiving." There is a

character named Aphasia about whom it is said, "Aphasia can guess until the cows come home."

21. Tallying fours/4s/fors/fores. As an academic footnote, film critic P. Adams Sitney explains the different kinds of *fors* and then totals them; his image is twice superimposed over itself as the totals are increased.

22. Mental Profumo L'Alito box is opened. It is empty. There is silence as in 5.

23. Curtain call and signature. A demonstration in homophonics. Snow holds up a cymbal, an orange and yellow, that is, a yellow object. A Snow-covered car follows as his signature.

24. Erratum. Additional "(for)e-fours-4s" are listed along with more credits in voice-over of those accidentally omitted from the initial count.

25. Addendum. It includes more sounds such as gargling, a baby cooing, vomiting, gagging, crying, and bird calls not previously heard in the film, a few tautological statements such as "that goes without saying," "in a manner of speaking," etc. ending with a brief shot of Dennis Young.

Filmography

All films are in 16mm.

A to Z (1956). 4 min. blue and white, silent.

New York Eye and Ear Control (1964). 34 min. b&w, sound.

Short Shave (1965). 4 min. b&w, sound.

Wavelength (1966-67). 45 min. colour, sound.

Standard Time (1967). 8 min. colour, sound.

⟵——————⟶ (1968-69). 52 min. colour, sound.

Dripping Water (1969). 10½ min. b&w, sound.
(Made in collaboration with Joyce Wieland.)

One Second in Montreal (1969). 26 min. b&w, silent.
(May be projected at sound speed, 17 min.)

Side Seat Paintings Slides Sound Film (1970). 20 min. colour, sound.

La Région Centrale (1970-71). 190 min. colour, sound.

Two Sides to Every Story (1974). 8 min. colour, sound. Two-screen.

"Rameau's Nephew" by Diderot (Thanx to Dennis Young) by Wilma Schoen (1972-74). 260 min. colour, sound.

Breakfast a.k.a. **Table Top Dolly** (1972 + 1976). 15 min. colour, sound.

Film Rental Agents

Films by Michael Snow are available for rental from the following sources:

The Canadian Filmmakers Distribution Centre
Suite 430
144 Front Street West
Toronto, Ontario

Co-opérative des cinéastes indépendants
3684 boulevard St-Laurent
Montreal, Quebec H2X 2V4

New York Filmmakers Cooperative
175 Lexington Avenue
New York 10016

The Museum of Modern Art Film Department
11 West 53rd Street
New York 10019

American Federation of Arts
41 East 65th Street
New York 10021

Castelli-Sonnabend
420 West Broadway
New York 10012

Grove Press
196 West Houston Street
New York

Canyon Cinema
Room 420
Industrial Centre Building
Sausalito,California 94965

London Filmmakers Cooperative
42 Gloucester Avenue
London NW1

Cinegate Film Distribution
Gate Cinema
87 Notting Hill Gate
London W11

Paris Films Coop
18 rue Montmartre
Paris 75001

Freunde Der Deutschen Kinematek Ev
1 West Berlin
Weiserstrasse 25

List of Photographic Works

Four to Five (1962)
Montage of photographs on board /3 30" x 48". Collection: Michael Snow, The Isaacs Gallery.

Un nuit d'amour (1963)
Photo-offset collage 26" x 25". Collection: Mr. and Mrs. G. Montague, Toronto.

Places (1964)
Photographs and collage 12" x 49". Collection: Michael Snow.

Announcementouncementment (1964)
Photo-offset 40" x 73½". Collection: Michael Snow, The Isaacs Gallery.

Carla Bley (TORONTO 20) (1965)
Photoprint /100 26" x 20". Collection: Michael Snow, The Isaacs Gallery.

Sleeve (1965)
Mixed media construction (photographs, paintings, reliefs, sculpture) 4 parts: 120" x 60" (wall piece), 60" x 20" (cut out figure), 79" x 72" x 8" (floor piece), 13" x 10" (piece for opposite wall). Collection: Michael Snow, The Isaacs Gallery.

Atlantic (1966)
Photographic prints, tinned metal sheet 70" x 96" x 12". Collection: The Art Gallery of Ontario, Toronto.

Snow Storm February 7, 1967 (1967)
Photographs, enamelled masonite 48" x 48". Collection: The National Gallery of Canada, Ottawa.

Amplast Inc. 359 Canal St. N.Y.C. (1967)
Photographs, vinyls, plexiglass 51" x 11½". Collection: Michael Snow, The Isaacs Gallery.

A Wooden Look (1969)
Colour photographs, felt tip pen, varnished plywood, engraved copper plaque 36½" x 96½". Collection: Musée des beaux-arts de Montréal.

Authorization (1969)
Black and white polaroid photographs, adhesive tape, mirror, metal 30" x 20". Collection: The National Gallery of Canada, Ottawa.

Press (1969)
Photographs, plastic 72" x 72" x 10". Collection: Dr. Sydney Wax, Toronto.

Tap (1969)
Photograph 40" x 72", and typewritten text 23¾" x 14", speaker, wire, sound. Collection: The National Gallery of Canada, Ottawa.

8 x 10 (1969)
80 black and white photographs laminated on aluminum, double-sided adhesive tape /2 113" x 181". Collection: Michael Snow, The Isaacs Gallery.

Untitled Slidelength (1969-71)
80 35mm slides, projector /3. Collection: The National Gallery of Canada, Ottawa.

SNOW SEEN

Sink (1970)
Colour photograph /3 15" x 18", 100 35mm slides, projector. Collection: The National Gallery of Canada, Marielle Mailhot, Montreal.

A Casing Shelved (1970)
Colour photograph on colour slide, cassette tape /3 14¼" x 10½". Collection: The National Gallery of Canada, Ottawa; The Canada Council Art Bank, Ottawa; Marielle Mailhot, Montreal.

Michael Snow/A Survey (1970)
Trade edition and limited edition /125. Published by The Isaacs Gallery and the Art Gallery of Ontario. Collection: The Isaacs Gallery.

Manual (1970)
Photo-offset lithograph 24" x 24" /135, available only with the limited edition *Michael Snow/A Survey*, and another edition /200. Collection: Michael Snow, The Isaacs Gallery.

Digest (1970)
Colour photographs, epoxy 12¼" x 13¾". Collection: Michael Snow, The Isaacs Gallery.

Projection (1970)
Photo-offset lithograph /50 20¼" x 24". Collection: Michael Snow, The Isaacs Gallery.

Venetian Blind (1970)
Colour photographs, framed /3 49½" x 92". Collection: Joanna Marsden; The Canada Council Art Bank, Ottawa; Michael Snow.

Crouch, Leap, Land (1970)
3 photographs 16¾" x 14¾", plexiglass, metal. Hangs 49" off the floor. Collection: Michael Snow, The Isaacs Gallery.

Halifax Harbour (1970)
Photograph 20" x 24". Collection: Michael Snow.

Of a Ladder (1971)
10 black and white photographs, laminated, each 11" x 14". Collection: The Albright-Knox Art Gallery, Buffalo.

Monocle (1972)
Photo montage 48" x 48". Collection: Barbara Jacob.

Photo Mural (1972)
20' x 30'. Collection: Brock University, St. Catharines, Ontario.

Glares (1973)
Photographs, glass, light, painted wood frame 58¾" x 39½". Collection: City Savings and Trust Co., Vancouver.

Inlet (1973)
Photo-offset and photograph /5 27½" x 40". Collection: Michael Snow, The Isaacs Gallery.

Chords (From the Artists' Jazz Band Suite) (1973)
Offset lithograph /100 24" x 24". Collection: Michael Snow, The Isaacs Gallery.

Morning in Holland (1969-74)
Photographs, adhesive tape, paper, enamel 49" x 48". Collection: The Canada Council Art Bank, Ottawa.

Midnight Blue (1973-74)
Wood, acrylic, colour photograph, wax 28½" x 26" x 5". Collection: Musée nationale d'art moderne, Centre Georges Pompidou, Paris.

LIST OF PHOTOGRAPHIC WORKS

Shutter Bugs (1973-74)
Colour photographs, plexiglass, wooden frame 22" x 28". Collection: The
   Canada Council Art Bank, Ottawa.

Field (1973-74)
Black and white photographs, painted wood frame 70½" x 66¾" (frame
   included). Collection: The National Gallery of Canada, Ottawa.

Log (1973-74)
Colour photograph, plexiglass 57" x 9½", log 109" x 9¼". Collection: The
   Canada Council Art Bank, Ottawa.

Red⁵ (1974)
Colour photograph, framed 25" x 31". Collection: The National Gallery of
   Canada, Ottawa.

Lobster (1974)
2 colour photographs on styrofoam, framed each 15½" x 18". Collection:
   Michael Snow, The Isaacs Gallery.

1956 (1974)
Offset lithograph and serigraph /100 22" x 27¾". Collection: The Isaacs
   Gallery.

Light Blues (1974)
Colour photographs, lamp, colour filter, frame 38" x 72". Collection: Canada
   Council Art Bank, Ottawa.

Cover and First Pages of Wittgenstein's Zettel (1975)
Photo-offset, *Impulse* Magazine, Fall 1975.

Cover to Cover (1975)
Book, published by the Nova Scotia College of Art and Design Press, and New
   York University Press.

Imposition (1976)
Colour photograph, wood frame /2 72" x 40". Collection: Peter Ludwig,
   Aachen; Marielle Mailhot, Montreal.

Plus Tard (1977)
25 colour photographs under plexiglass, wood frames each 34" x 42½".
   Collection: The National Gallery of Canada, Ottawa.

P.29 (1979)
Colour photograph and acrylic paint / 2 10½" 20". Collection: Michael
   Snow, The Isaacs Gallery.

Traces (1977)
Colour photograph, wood frame 46½" x 40" (includes frame). Collection:
   The Canada Council Art Bank, Ottawa.

Multiplication Table (1977)
Laminated colour photograph 43" x 74". Collection: Michael Snow, The
   Isaacs Gallery.

Wild Flower Bed (1977)
Colour photographs, cloth, wood frame 49½" x 97½". Collection: Michael
   Snow, The Isaacs Gallery.

Painting (Closing the Drum Book) (1978)
Colour photograph, wood frame, wood base 46" x 46" x 39" x 43½"
   (irregular sides), 8¾" high. Collection: Marielle Mailhot, Montreal.

Dispersed Photo Works (1978)
21 pieces from 7' x 6' to 16" x 28". Collection: Government of Canada
   Building, North York, Ontario.

175

Chair Back (1979)
Laminated colour photograph and acrylic paint, wood frame 87¼" x 59⅝". Collection: The Council House Collection, S.C. Johnson & Son Incorporated, Racine, Wisconsin.

Times (1979)
Colour photograph, wood frame 69¾" x 67¾". Collection: The Milwaukee Art Gallery.

Watercolours (1979)
Colour photograph and acrylic 16½" x 27½". Collection: Marielle Montreal.

Door (1979)
Photograph, wood frame /2   90" x 47¼" x 6". Collection: Musée des beaux-arts de Montréal and The Art Gallery, The University of Guelph.

X 60 (1979)
Colour photograph 38⅝" x 62½". Collection: Michael Snow, The Isaacs Gallery.

Bees Behaving on Blue (1979)
Colour photograph /3 31" x 30½". Collection: Michael Snow, The Isaacs Gallery.

Blue Blazes (1979)
Colour photograph 34½" x 28½". Collection: Michael Snow, The Isaacs Gallery.

Was Red (1979)
Colour photograph 79" x 27⅛". Collection: Michael Snow, The Isaacs Gallery.

Going Up (1979)
Colour photograph 28½" x 12⅜". Collection: Gail Hutchinson, Toronto.

Diamond (1979)
Colour photograph 33½" x 33½". Collection: The Isaacs Gallery.

iris-IRIS (1979)
Colour photograph, collage and painting. Two panels, each 48" x 47". Collection: The Art Gallery of Ontario.

Shade (1979)
Photograph 62" x 70". Collection: The Canada Council Art Bank, Ottawa.

Flight Stop (1979)
60 units, fiberglass, photographs 105' x 65' x 55'. The Eaton Centre, Toronto.

Exam (1979)
Photo-offset print /120 100 for limited edition of book *High School*. Collection: Michael Snow, The Isaacs Gallery.

Bibliography

Alloway, Lawrence. "Systemic Painting." In *Minimal Art: A Critical Anthology*, pp. 37-60. Edited by Gregory Battock. New York: Dutton, 1968.

Andrew, Dudley. "Critics: André Bazin." *Film Comment* 9, no. 2 (March-April 1973), pp. 64-68.

Auchterlone, Bill. "Review—Artfilms." *Arts Magazine* (October 1975), p. 1.

Bazin, André. *What is Cinema?* 2 vols. Translated by Hugh Gray. Berkeley: University of California Press, 1967-72.

Bell, Clive. *Art.* 1913. Reprint. New York: Capricorn Books, 1958.

Brakhage, Stan. *The Brakhage Lectures: George Méliès, David Wark Griffith, Carl Theodore Dreyer, Sergei Eisenstein.* Chicago: Good Lion Press at the Art Institute of Chicago, 1972.

_____. *Metaphors on Vision*, title given to entire issue of *Film Culture*, no. 30 (Fall 1963).

_____. *A Moving Picture Giving and Taking Book.* West Newbury, Mass.: Frontier Press, 1971.

Brooks, Cleanth. *Modern Poetry and the Tradition.* n.p., University of North Carolina Press, 1939.

_____. *The Well Wrought Urn.* New York: Reynal and Hitchcock, 1947.

Burch, Noël. *Theory of Film Practice.* Translated by Helen R. Lane. New York: Praeger, 1973.

Burch, Noël, and Dana, Jorge. "Propositions." *Afterimage* (London), no. 5 (Spring 1974), pp. 40-66.

"The Camera and the Spectator: Michael Snow in Discussion with John DuCane." *Studio International* 186, no. 960 (November 1973), pp. 177-79.

Cavell, Stanley. *The World Viewed: Reflections on the Ontology of Film.* New York: Viking Press, 1971.

Coplans, John, with contributions by Mekas, Jonas and Tomkins, Calvin. *Andy Warhol.* London: Weidenfeld and Nicolson, n.d.

_____. *Serial Imagery.* Greenwich, Conn.: New York Graphic Society in association with The Pasadena Art Museum, 1968.

Cornwell, Regina. "Michael Snow." In *Projected Images*, pp. 26-33. Minneapolis: Walker Art Center, 1974.

_____. "Michael Snow: *Cover to Cover* and Back . . ." *Studio International* 191, no. 980 (March-April 1976), pp. 193-97.

Diderot, Denis. *Rameau's Nephew and Other Works.* Translated by Jacques Barzun and Ralph H. Bowen. New York: Bobbs-Merrill, 1964.

Edinburgh International Film Festival. Program Notes on *"Rameau's Nephew."* Edinburgh, 1975, pp. 1-6.

Erlich, Victor. *Russian Formalism: History-Doctrine.* 3rd ed. The Hague: Mouton, 1969.

Farber, Manny. *Negative Space.* New York: Praeger, 1971.

Film-Makers' Cooperative Catalogue No. 5. New York: Harry Gantt Publishers for Film-Makers' Cooperative, 1971.

Fried, Michael. *Three American Painters: Kenneth Noland, Jules Olitski, Frank Stella.* Cambridge, Mass.: Fogg Art Museum, Harvard, 1965.

_____. "Shape as Form: Frank Stella's New Painting." *Artforum* 5, no. 3 (November 1966), pp. 18-27.

_____. "Toward a Supreme Fiction: Genre and Beholder in the Art Criticism of Diderot and His Contemporaries." *New Literary History* 6, no. 3 (Spring 1975), pp. 543-84.

Fry, Roger. *Vision and Design.* Cleveland: Meridian Books, World Publishing Co., 1966.

Gray, Christopher. *Cubist Aesthetic Theories.* Baltimore: Johns Hopkins Press, 1967.

Greenberg, Clement. "After Abstract Expressionism." *Art International* 6, no. 13 (October 1962), pp. 24-32.

_____. *Art and Culture: Critical Essays.* Boston: Beacon Press, 1968.

_____. "Modernist Painting." *Arts Yearbook* 4 (1961), pp. 103-08.

_____. "The Necessity of 'Formalism.'" *New Literary History* 3, no. 1 (Autumn 1971), pp. 171-75.

_____. "Problems of Criticism II: Complaints of an Art Critic." *Artforum* 6, no. 2 (October 1967), pp. 38-39.

_____. *Avant-Garde Attitudes: New Art in the Sixties.* Sydney, Australia: University of Sydney, 1969.

Hartman, Geoffrey H. *Beyond Formalism: Literary Essays 1958-1970.* New Haven, Conn.: Yale University Press, 1971.

Hassan, Ihab. "POSTmodernISM." *New Literary History* 3, no. 1 (Autumn 1971), pp. 5-30.

Hawkes, Terence. *Structuralism and Semiotics.* Berkeley: University of California Press, 1977.

Hayum, Andrée. "Information or Illusion: An Interview with Michael Snow." *Review* 72, no. 7 (Winter 1972), pp. 55-60.

"Hollis Frampton Interviewed by Michael Snow." *Film Culture,* no. 48-49 (Winter-Spring 1970), pp. 6-12.

Hulme, T.E. *Speculations: Essays on Humanism and the Philosophy of Art.* Edited by Herbert Read. New York: Harcourt, Brace and Co., n.d.

Jacobs, Lewis, ed. *Introduction to the Art of the Movies.* New York: Farrar, Straus & Cudahy, 1960.

Jaffé, Hans L.C., ed. *De Stijl.* Translated by R.R. Symonds, Mary Whitall, et al. New York: Abrams, 1971.

Josephs, Herbert. *Diderot's Dialogue of Language and Gesture: Le Neveu de Rameau.* n.p., Ohio University Press, 1969.

Koch, Stephen. *Stargazer: Andy Warhol's World and His Films.* New York: Praeger, 1973.

Kracauer, Siegfried. *Theory of Film: The Redemption of Physical Reality.* New York: Oxford University Press, 1965.

Krieger, Murray. *The New Apologists for Poetry.* Bloomington, Ind.: Indiana University Press, 1963.

Kubler, George. *The Shape of Time: Remarks on the History of Things.* New Haven, Conn.: Yale University Press, 1968.

BIBLIOGRAPHY

Léger, Fernand. "A New Realism—The Object." *The Little Review* (Paris) 11, no. 2 (Winter 1926), pp. 7-8.

Lemon, Lee T., and Reis, Marion J., trans. *Russian Formalist Criticism: Four Essays*. Lincoln, Neb.: Bison Book, University of Nebraska Press, 1965.

"The Life and Times of Michael Snow." *Take One* 3, no. 3 (January-February 1971, published April 7, 1972), pp. 6-12. (Snow interviewed by Joe Medjuck.)

Locke, John W., "Michael Snow's *La Région Centrale*." *Artforum* 12, no. 3 (November 1973), pp. 66-71; and *Artforum* 12, no. 4 (December 1973), pp. 66-72.

Malevich, Kasimir. *Essays on Art*. 2 vols. Edited by Troels Anderson. Translated by Xenia Glowacki-Prus and Arnold McMillin. Copenhagen: Borgen, 1969.

_____. "'Suprematism' from *The Non-Objective World*." In *Theories of Modern Art: A Source Book by Artists and Critics*, edited by Herschel Chipp, pp. 341-46. Berkeley: University of California Press, 1970.

Mascelli, Joseph V. and Miller, Arthur, eds. *American Cinematographer Manual*. 2nd ed. Hollywood: American Society of Cinematographers, 1967.

Matejka, Ladislav and Pomorska, Krystyna, eds. *Readings in Russian Poetics: Formalist and Structuralist Views*. Cambridge, Mass.: Massachusetts Institute of Technology, 1971.

Mekas, Jonas. "Movie Journal." *Village Voice*, November 14, 1974, p. 97.

_____. "A Note on Michael Snow, Written in a Minnesota Snowstorm." *Take One* 3, no. 3 (January-February 1971, published April 7, 1972), p. 12.

[_____]"Sixth Independent Film Award." *Film Culture*, no. 33 (Summer 1964), p. 1.

Mekas, Jonas and Sitney, P. Adams. "Conversations with Michael Snow." *Film Culture*, no. 46 (Autumn 1967, published belatedly October 1968), pp. 1-4.

Merleau-Ponty, Maurice. *Sense and Non-Sense*. Translated by Hubert L. Dreyfus and Patricia A. Dreyfus. Evanston, Ill.: Northwestern University Press, 1971.

"Michael Snow in Conversation with John DuCane." *Light*, no. 1. (London, n.d.), no pagination.

Michelson, Annette. "Books." *Artforum* 6, no. 10 (Summer 1968), pp. 67-71.)

_____. "Film and the Radical Aspiration." *Film Culture*, no. 42 (Fall 1966), pp. 34-42, 136.

_____. "Toward Snow: Part I." *Artforum* 9, no. 10 (June 1971), pp. 30-37.

Nichols, Bill, ed. *Movies and Methods*. Berkeley: University of California Press, 1976.

Ortega y Gasset, José. *The Dehumanization of Art: And Other Writings on Art and Culture*. New York: Doubleday, 1956.

Panofsky, Erwin. "Style and Medium in the Motion Pictures." In *Film: An Anthology*, edited by Daniel Talbot, pp. 15-32. New York: Simon and Schuster, 1959.

Peckham, Morse. *Art and Pornography: An Experiment in Explanation*. New York: Harper and Row, 1971.

_____. *Man's Rage for Chaos: Biology, Behavior and the Arts*. New York: Schocken, 1969.

Poggioli, Renato. *Theory of the Avant-Garde*. Translated by Gerald Fitzgerald. Cambridge, Mass.: Belknap Press, Harvard University Press, 1968.

Pomorska, Krystyna. *Russian Formalist Theory and Its Poetic Ambiance*. The Hague: Mouton, 1968.

Ransom, John Crowe. *The New Criticism*. Norfolk, Conn.: New Directions, 1941.

_____. *The World's Body*. New York: Scribner, 1938.

Robbe-Grillet, Alain. *For a New Novel: Essays on Fiction*. Translated by Richard Howard. New York: Grove Press, 1965.

Sennett, Richard. *The Fall of Public Man*. New York: Knopf, 1977.

Sitney, P. Adams. "The Idea of Morphology." *Film Culture*, nos. 53-54-55 (Spring 1972), pp.1-24.

_____. "Structural Film. " *Film Culture*, no. 47 (Summer 1969), pp. 1-10.

_____. *Visionary Film: The American Avant-Garde*. New York: Oxford University Press, 1974.

Sitney, P. Adams, ed. *Film Culture Reader*. New York: Praeger, 1970.

Smith, Brydon, ed. *Michael Snow/Canada*. Ottawa: National Gallery of Canada, 1970. (A catalogue for the Thirty-fifth International Biennial Exhibition of Art, Venice, 1970.)

Snow, Michael. "Letter." *Film Culture*, no. 46 (Autumn 1967, published belatedly October 1968), pp. 4-5.

_____. *Michael Snow/A Survey*. Toronto: Art Gallery of Ontario in collaboration with the Isaacs Gallery, 1970.

_____. "Passage." *Artforum* 10, no. 1 (September 1971), p. 63.

_____. "*La Région Centrale*." *Film Culture*, no. 52 (Spring 1971), pp. 58-63.

_____. "A Statement on *Wavelength* for the Experimental Film Festival of Knokke-le-Zoute." *Film Culture*, no. 46 (Autumn 1967, published belatedly October 1968), p. 1.

Sontag, Susan. *Against Interpretation: And Other Essays*. New York: Dell, 1970.

Stallman, Robert Wooster, comp. *Critiques and Essays in Criticism: 1920-1948*. New York: Ronald Press, 1949.

Tate, Allen. *Reason in Madness: Critical Essays*. New York: Putnam, 1941.

Taubin, Amy. "Doubled Visions." *October*, no. 4 (Fall 1977), pp. 33-42.

Théberge, Pierre, ed. *About 30 Works by Michael Snow*. Ottawa: National Gallery of Canada, 1972. (A catalogue for the Snow exhibition at the Center for Inter-American Relations in New York City in 1972.)

Tomkins, Calvin. *The Bride and the Bachelors: Five Masters of the Avant-Garde*. New York: Viking Press, 1968.

Tuchman, Maurice, ed. *American Art of the Sixties*. Greenwich, Conn.: New York Graphic Society, 1967.

BIBLIOGRAPHY

Wellek, René, and Warren, Austin. *Theory of Literature*. New York: Harvest Book, Harcourt, Brace and World, 1956.

Wollen, Peter. *Signs and Meaning in the Cinema*. New and enlarged ed. Bloomington, Ind.: University of Indiana Press, 1972.

Youngblood, Gene. *Expanded Cinema*. New York: Dutton, 1970.

Index

Numbers in boldface refer to illustrations